Changing The Conversation

21st Club presents a collection of insights for football club boardrooms

"Fresh, analytical and thought-provoking."
(Dan Jones, Lead Partner, Deloitte Sports Business Group)

"They always make me think."
(Tony Scholes, CEO, Stoke City)

"Short, sharp and thoughtful."
(Simon Wilson, Director of Football Services, City Football Group)

"Insight communicated effectively to decision makers."
(Ian Lynam, Partner, Joint Head of Sport, Charles Russell Speechlys LLP)

"One of the best around for stimulating thought."
(Howard Wilkinson, Chairman, League Managers Association)

"Keeps you thinking about best practice when developing a football club."
(José Riestra López, Director of Football, Club Santos Laguna)

"A must for key decision-makers to challenge conventional thinking."
(David Sheepshanks CBE, Chairman, St George's Park Advisory Board)

"Bringing common sense to the football world."
(Grétar Steinsson, Technical Director, Fleetwood Town F.C.)

"Cutting edge insight."
(Daniel Geey, Partner, Sheridans Sport Group)

"Clear thinking and informed analysis."
(David Heller, Investor, Crystal Palace, Philadelphia 76ers)

"I always read whatever they write."
(Sean Ingle, Senior Sports Writer, Guardian News & Media)

"A great tool to have in the box."
(Les Reed, Executive Director of Football, Southampton F.C.)

"Pioneering insight that every ownership group should lean upon."
(Mike Forde, Founder, Ingenio Management)

"Fun to read!"
(Robert Eenhoorn, CEO, AZ Alkmaar)

Contents

II: Talent

III: Performance

Acknowledgements

The creation of this book has been a collaborative project between the 21st Club team and our network of colleagues and contributors.

21st Club's Omar Chaudhuri, Blake Wooster and Ben Marlow have produced the majority of insights featured in this book. However, we would like to extend our thanks for the valuable contributions from Ian Lynam, Mark Taylor and Richard Whittall, all of whom have written with great enthusiasm and wisdom on their chosen subjects.

Thanks also to Chris Mann for managing the editorial process, Elizabeth Marlow for her work on the cover design, and to Opta Sports for supplying performance data.

Introduction

The story of football over the last two decades has been one of commercialisation, expansion and unprecedented wealth. Bankrolled by colossal broadcast revenues, football has become more lucrative than ever before, but that success has come at a cost.

As a handful of elite clubs have been transformed into multi-billion dollar organisations, the majority have been frozen out as the gap between the game's haves and have-nots has grown at an extraordinary rate. It would be natural to presume that football's balance of power is binary; that it is as advantageous to the wealthiest clubs as it is an impediment to the less fortunate. There is truth in that, but in reality both groups are faced with different but equally exacting sets of challenges.

For wealthy clubs, the question is how they can differentiate their strategy to achieve competitive advantage in a world where money is no object for themselves or their rivals. For clubs further down the ladder, the test is to find innovative ways to tip the odds in their favour; their challenge is to level the playing field and compete despite the financial imbalance.

21st Club exists to *change the conversation* by challenging received wisdom and providing objective insights to bring clarity to decision-making. This approach helps football clubs to explore new ways of thinking about key issues such as strategy, culture, succession planning, talent development, recruitment and innovation. By applying intelligence to data and contextualising it to specific challenges, the unique insights yielded by objective thinking enable clubs to gain an advantage through innovation rather than expenditure.

Over the last few years we've been sharing our views on these topics via our Evolution blog. This book celebrates the recent publication of our 100th post by bringing together a selection of the most popular articles and grouping them into four broad categories:

1. Strategy
2. Talent
3. Performance, and
4. Planning

Presenting stories, case studies and analytical methods that demonstrate the value of our approach, this book enables football club boardrooms – and decision-makers across a range of industries – to help their organisations find true competitive advantage.

Of course, there is nothing stopping you from reading the posts in their original form on the 21st Club website, but here they are grouped by topic and curated with a logical flow. Whether you're travelling on business or just taking five minutes out of your day to clear your head, each bite-sized insight is designed so you can read it in less than the time it takes to drink your morning coffee.

Our hope is that this book becomes a useful point of reference and a source of impartial insight during your daily decision-making processes, helping you to make a positive difference as you shape the future of your organisation.

I: STRATEGY

The Smart Boardroom...

Sets the right pre-season expectations, based on the right metrics.

Implements long-term strategies, rather than relying on short-term tactics.

Creates accountability around the club's philosophy, to ensure that progress and success are measured against relevant KPIs.

Recognises the importance of measuring performance, not just results.

Knows that the wage bill doesn't automatically equal success, and that innovation can be the differentiator.

Appreciates that success in the transfer market is often no more certain than the toss of a coin, so nudges the odds in their favour by creating simple recruitment guidelines and identifying likely future stars from their own academy.

Recruits a new manager or head coach according to the club's existing structure and philosophy, instead of giving the new boss carte blanche.

Has contingency plans in place for when things inevitably don't go to plan.

Doesn't panic on transfer deadline day and enjoys the freedom to do nothing.

Understands that listening and engaging with fans is the key to success.

We live in a short term world, but sometimes we need to see the advantage in taking the long way round.

Multi Duce, Una Voce

It's no secret that a transfer strategy controlled by the manager, as is prevalent in English football, has certain weaknesses. However, while a more diverse range of voices can help a club to make more reasoned decisions, it is equally true that once a decision has been made, the club must speak with one voice in its implementation.

To enable a unified approach to strategic decisions, a strong chain of command with clearly delegated responsibilities must be established and embedded within a club's culture. There can be no room for uncertainty or mixed messages. Players and their agents must have one interface to deal with on all transfer matters, whether that is the CEO or a Director of Football. The sideline involvement of a superior, such as the Chairman or Owner, has the potential to undermine the negotiator's position and can be a major threat to potential deals.

Equally, twin-track discussions between the agent and the football side can easily be turned to the agent's advantage. This situation is created by the contrasting incentives of those involved in the talks; the CEO being responsible for the club's long-term financial and organisational sustainability, while the manager thinks in terms of winning the next match.

The absence of a clear chain of command is more common in football than it might appear. This issue is highlighted in those deals that see agents negotiate directly with each of the owner, chairman, manager and commercial department. Needless to say, it becomes too easy for the agent to divide and conquer, manipulating the process to his and his player's advantage.

An understanding of leverage is essential at the outset of any negotiation. In the post-Bosman world, the deck is generally stacked in favour of the player. However, intelligent and well-run clubs can address this imbalance in a number of ways. Establishing a clear chain of command is a good place to start.

Will This Help Us Win?

Before signing a new player, investing in new technology, applying analytics to your process, or accepting that meeting, ask yourself and your colleagues one question: "Will this help us win?" If the answer is ambiguous then tell those asking for budget or time to go back to the drawing board.

Sometimes we lose sight of the end game, which is to achieve competitive advantage and, ultimately, to win. 'Winning', of course, needn't necessarily mean the next game. It depends on your club's objectives and might relate to various goals, including the development of talent, profit generation, community initiatives, or exceeding long-term expectations.

But if it's not contributing to winning, then it's really not worth it.

How Do We Know This Works?

As recently as the late 19th century, some physicians were convinced that practices such as bloodletting were effective methods for treating certain illnesses. Nowadays, we know such treatments to be useless or even damaging, but it wasn't until people started challenging 'expert' opinion that change finally came about.

In that instance, change was the result of people asking a simple question: how do we know this works? That question encouraged the creation of hypotheses and trials which led to the production of verifiable results.

There are many areas of football clubs where conventional wisdom also goes unchallenged. How do we know this works? "Because I know it works," might be a typical response, but the evidence provided often overlooks significant flaws.

For example, until recently we had assumed that the positive relationship between spending and success was clear and instructive. However, more recently we have learnt that we've ignored some crucial lessons from history and that the correlation is not so clear.

Some questions are more obvious than others. Are we sure our bonuses truly incentivise our players? Do we know if our scouting process unearths the right talent? Does our approach to identifying head coaches give us the most suitable candidates?

In science, these questions would be tackled with controlled experiments, but this is impractical in the fast-moving world of sport. Therefore, it often takes a leap of faith to go beyond the question and try something that goes against the grain.

How do we know this works? "Because all the available evidence suggests that doing this will shift the odds in our favour."

The Meaning of Aggression

Professional sport is full of buzzwords and banalities, perhaps the most common of which is the demand to be "positive" or "aggressive" in approach.

In an interview with the Guardian in early 2016, two-time Wimbledon champion Andy Murray highlighted the dangerous oversimplifications such language can lead to:

"A lot of commentators say you have to be more aggressive. Does that mean you hit the ball harder, or play closer to the line, or serve and volley? Does it mean you have to stand closer to the baseline? At the highest level you can't just say: 'Be aggressive.' You need a proper strategy. José Mourinho wouldn't send his team out against Barcelona and just say: 'Be more aggressive.' It's a lot more complex playing the best in the world."

As Murray suggests, among players and coaches it's widely accepted that strategies need to be coherently formed and articulated. However, at boardroom level – where there is less visibility and therefore less obvious accountability – there is still the tendency to slip into generic turns of phrase.

This particularly applies when devising and communicating an overarching philosophy. We'll often hear of a club's commitment to "developing young players" or "playing exciting football" without knowing how those notions are translated into a coherent strategy.

This is where data can be our best friend, a means to assess and validate both what we can and cannot see with our own eyes. It is also a way to create joined-up thinking, as points of dispute can be clarified and agreed through numbers. 'Exciting football' may require a certain level of expected goals per game, while 'youth development' might be measured as a proportion of homegrown minutes in the first team. These are quantifiable metrics.

So while "aggression" and "excitement" may be starting points for discussion, they are certainly not the basis for a strategy. For that, objective measures can help to crystallise boardroom thinking and create true accountability.

The Football View vs The Business View

The idea that football clubs should be run like businesses is becoming increasingly fashionable in certain areas of the sport. While it is true that new regulation and changing attitudes have fostered a greater focus on the adoption of corporate practices, football remains totally unlike many other industries.

Many football clubs have internal struggles between the 'football' and the 'business' views. This conflict can permeate through the entire organisation, negatively influencing decisions on when to sell players, how to measure success, or how to grow the club. In many cases compromise is sub-optimal, or common ground non-existent.

Most damaging, however, is when the two sides fail to see things from each other's perspective. Countless key figures at clubs have been undermined by blind spots that eventually lead to decisions that disregard their position.

The most effective clubs have football and business people who understand the implications of each other's decisions. Both realise that a young player's contract renewal depends on a commercial deal being signed, or that long-term plans have a need for short-term results.

Football clubs may need to be run more like traditional businesses in some respects, but they needn't reject the realities of the sport. When the football and business views operate in silos, it is ultimately the club that loses out.

When Objectives Are Not Aligned

In new relationships there can sometimes be a discrepancy in the couple's respective intentions. While one may have long-term aspirations about settling down, buying a house and starting a family, the other may be looking no further than the next date.

In a sport where managers lose their jobs with alarming regularity, it's easy to wonder if something similar is going on in football. It certainly seems that many clubs suffer from a disconnect between their strategic objectives and the performance evaluation of those picking the team.

Crudely, there are two types of approach in the evaluation of managers:

> Strategy 1: Evaluate the manager (or head coach) on short-term results alone, or

> Strategy 2: Appraise on results and long-term goals.

Strategy 2 may be preferable in most instances, but sometimes clubs need to focus on Strategy 1 to afford the time required to indulge in long-term thinking. The issue comes when a club says that it is committed to the long-term, when in reality they hire and fire on the back of a few poor results. In our relationship analogy, it's akin to both partners claiming to want commitment, yet one straying to have a one-night stand.

Interestingly, when we looked at which of the top clubs in England had given the most minutes to young players over each of the past six seasons, we noticed that half had disposed of their manager during the campaign. This points to a misalignment of objectives and a broader issue around talent development. Surely it is unrealistic to expect managers to give youth a chance when they are invariably judged on results. Younger players need time to find their feet, and that's often more time than clubs are prepared to give.

For clubs wanting to find the right balance between short- and long-term priorities, the introduction of a balance scorecard (BSC) approach might be the solution. Applied in other industries, the BSC is a performance management tool that helps organisations balance their strategic agenda with short-term objectives.

In football, the BSC could evaluate achievement against the following KPIs:

- Results: winning football matches or achieving points.

- Performance: assessing the club's underlying on-field performance.

- Productivity: the number of club-trained players in the first team, or the percentage of minutes played by homegrown players.

In order to avoid conflict and achieve sustainable success, football's leaders must endeavour to align the targets of the manager with the objectives of the club. A manager who has incentives based on both results and productivity is more likely to give youth a chance. We can't blame those who don't if they are measured on results alone.

Football's Failure in Philosophy

In any ordinary organisation, philosophical alignment is a key factor in success. If the workers on the shop floor can endorse the vision of the organisation, then head office has a greater chance of achieving it. It is for this reason that much time, energy and money is spent on communicating that vision to those that will help deliver it.

But football clubs are not ordinary organisations. In football, stakeholders are often focused on the tangible business of the next game, and so decisions may contradict any embedded philosophy in the hope of achieving short-term results. Indeed, few clubs successfully implement a philosophy or ethos that survives a poor run of form, with emotive impulses undermining long-term thinking.

The most obvious example of this is in the recruitment of managers, where new hires often bear no resemblance in approach or outlook to their predecessors. Despite this, they are empowered to fundamentally change the club to suit their own style, even though probability suggests that the team will have a new coach within a year. This can result in previously productive players being consigned to the bench, or worse, the shop window. There are only a few clubs that have undergone extensive managerial change and emerged unscathed, with the team retaining a consistent style and core group of players.

When a philosophy successfully permeates an entire club, the rewards can be far-reaching. Embedding a philosophy can align a club in its approach to transfers, tactics, youth development and managerial recruitment, with the following benefits:

- Low player and staff turnover as new staff adapt to the club rather than the other way around. Those who don't buy into the club's philosophy will be identified during the recruitment process and not offered a job.

- Reduction in 'key person risk', as individual roles become subordinate to the club's ethos. This gives the club a better chance of surviving the departure of influential members of staff.

- Enhancement of the club's negotiating position as it becomes more confident in knowing exactly what it is looking for.

- Better results. If playing staff buy in to the club's ethos they will become emotionally invested in the club's success. This produces better performances and better results over time.

In principle, the benefits of a suitable and intelligent philosophy arc clear. The challenge for clubs is holding their nerve when results are not forthcoming. For this to happen, they must define a clear vision in which people can believe and commit to embedding it for the long-term.

The First Guy Through the Wall

John Henry fixes a tired Billy Beane in the eye. The Oakland Athletics' recent play-off defeat weighs heavily on Beane, made heavier still by the steady stream of pundits queuing up to discredit his methods on the basis of that season-ending defeat.

Henry begins to reel off statistics from the A's extraordinary season; the players lost, the games won, how little each win cost, the famous streak. In that poignant scene from *Moneyball*, he implores Beane to block out the noise and to understand and appreciate what has been achieved. Henry empathises with a wonderful line:

"I know you're taking it in the teeth out there, but the first guy through the wall always gets bloodied. Always."

Innovation will always meet with opposition from those accustomed to doing things a certain way. Such criticism can, and often does, confound objective evidence as if to suggest that, for some incumbents, worse is better than different.

Ultimately, if you want to do something differently, you have to be 'all in'. You have to be prepared for opposition and ready to hold your nerve if things don't go your way.

Not all innovations work of course, but you will only know the outcome for certain once your new approach has been given sufficient time to succeed. A bad decision or a run of bad luck does not necessarily mean that the whole approach is broken, but too often they are used as an excuse for a return to the status quo. In being ready to avoid such a reversal, you have to see it through, for better or worse.

The incentive to take such risks is clear: if you don't, someone else will. As Henry says in the denouement of his speech at Fenway Park:

"Anybody who is not tearing down their team and rebuilding it using your model? They're dinosaurs. They'll be sitting on their ass on the sofa in October watching the Boston Red Sox win the World Series."

In football as in baseball, if you fail to keep up, you'll get left behind.

A Successful Flop

"Someone once bet me I couldn't clear a stuffed leather chair. Not only did I lose the bet, I also broke my hand in the crash landing."

If asked to attribute those words, I suspect few would turn to a list of past Olympic jumping champions for inspiration, yet they are the words of Dick Fosbury, 1968 Olympic high jump gold medallist, recalling an unfortunate college incident. The 'Fosbury Flop', the technique the American used to win gold, has since become the dominant method in high jumping and is known the world over. What is less clear, however, is what led to its creation.

The truth is, the young Fosbury was not very good at high jumping. His failure to win that college bet is just one of many that litter the path of his early career. It was his consistent failure using the prevailing techniques of the time that forced Fosbury to try something different. His failure gave him reason to innovate.

This inability to compete has also bred innovation in football. FC Midtjylland, the 2015 Danish champions, are the most recent example of a club thinking differently. Their innovative approach, focused on set pieces and the use of analytics in the transfer market, has helped them to compete, and win, against more established clubs with far greater resources.

The key difference between these particular success stories, however, is in the longevity of the innovations. In high jump, every gold medal since 1972 has been won using the Fosbury Flop. Fosbury's innovation has become the new normal. In football, however, FC Midtjylland are verging on unique as very few have followed their lead. It is still early days, but will other clubs be required to fail before the Midtjylland way becomes ubiquitous?

The lesson here is that difficult situations, while troublesome in the short-term, can give rise to innovations that create lasting value.

Changing Lanes

As anyone who has ever taken a taxi in New York will tell you, weaving back and forth between freeway lanes is unlikely to get you to your destination any faster.

The same is true in football, where we're often too quick to make changes when things are seemingly not going our way. For example, clubs in the five major European leagues average a change of head coach every 12 months, that despite the data telling us that such change has little impact on the long-term performance of the team.

By all means give yourself room to manoeuvre if the current plan isn't working. But before you change lanes make sure that you've taken the time to truly understand where the prevailing course will take you.

When you know where you're headed and why, often the more courageous move is to pick a lane and stick to it. Even when it seems like the other lanes are moving faster.

The Freedom to Do Nothing

The January transfer window throws up a lot of important questions for football clubs. Buy or sell? Stick or twist? What players do we need? Who can we trust?

In the modern world of online scouting technologies and global connectivity, we have more choices and more resources at our disposal than ever before.

The problem with shopping in January is that you're essentially in the market for what everyone else is buying. The law of supply and demand means you're likely to pay a premium.

A cynical way of looking at the January transfer window would be to see it as a trap, a media facade based on herd dynamics. It's not that straightforward, however. Injuries happen and players may want to move on; sometimes you really do need that player.

But consider this statistic before bringing new faces into the dressing room:

Since 2009/10, 54% of Premier League signings made in January have failed to play more than 50% of available league minutes after joining the club; exactly the same proportion as the players who were already there in the first place.

With this in mind, a better question to ask during the transfer window might be, "What if the answer lies in the room?"

Is Doing Nothing, Something?

If there's an off-field parallel to the penalty shootout, it's the month of January. The arrival of the transfer window coupled with contract renewals and perhaps decisions about the manager's future make it a month of high-pressure choices, much like the choices our players must make from the spot.

The results in both scenarios are transparent: success or failure. For players, actions are judged in the moment, whereas boardroom decisions typically take a few months before a result can be determined.

Off the field, we would all like to think that we're acting in the best interests of our team. In a shootout, however, there's one key actor who doesn't do what's best: the goalkeeper. The goalkeeper generally dives to one side, doing so far more frequently than would be optimal given the number of kicks down the middle of the goal. A group of economists think they know why and have labelled the phenomenon 'action bias'.

When questioned, some goalkeepers claimed they would feel worse letting in a penalty after standing in the middle than they would if they attempted a dive. Standing in the middle, which is a deviation from the norm, makes a goalkeeper look like he's not making an effort. He feels compelled to act and does so by diving to one side.

This can apply off the field, too. Sometimes we feel the urge to do something which at least makes us look like we're making an effort. New signings fill column inches and generate excitement among fans, but perhaps our injured players are returning soon and we might be best served by filling the bench with young prospects. A change of manager might bring fresh ideas, but is the underlying performance of the current manager a cause for optimism?

It takes courage and know-how to step back, assess the fundamentals and not make changes for the sake of it. When the norm is to buy players and switch managers, it's hard to do nothing, but sometimes doing nothing is the way to succeed.

When Does Stability Become Complacency?

Through the Elite Player Performance Plan, the completion of St George's Park and various Financial Fair Play measures, English football has recently helped create and been subject to a wave of governance designed to encourage clubs to be stable and sustainable. In this changing environment, it is more important than ever that clubs establish strong processes for succession planning on and off the field.

In the early stages of the 2014/15 Premier League and Championship seasons, 74% of minutes were played by players who represented the same club in the previous campaign. That's equivalent to around 8 of the starting 11. Interestingly, respective league champions Manchester City (91%), Leicester City (87%) and Wolves (91%) ranked highly in the list of teams who largely retained the same core, suggesting a conscious decision to reward their players and maintain the status quo. Meanwhile, clubs chasing the Premier League title such as Liverpool (66%) and Chelsea (73%) made – or were forced to make – more changes. In the Championship, the churn was even greater, with an average of just 68% minutes being played by last season's squad.

Organisational stability can foster engagement and improve performance; people know where they stand. On the other hand, disruption can be beneficial. In his book *Hunger in Paradise*, 21st Club co-founder Rasmus Ankersen suggests that successful companies should think differently in order to avoid the rut of complacency. Ankersen suggests that "if it ain't broken, consider breaking it", and recognises that it's often harder to innovate when you have something to lose.

In all walks of life, we tend to focus more on how to achieve success and less about how to sustain it. There is no hidden formula in football, it simply comes down to optimal squad turnover from one season to the next. In planning for the future, clubs must try to find the balance between constancy and complacency. Every club's context will be different, meaning that the only true constant is that every club should be focusing on continuity and long-term succession planning.

The German Penalty Theory

At most football clubs, it is typically a small collection of individuals that takes the blame for a run of poor results. This pressure can make effective decision-making all the more difficult, but a tale about German penalty takers can teach us something about how to handle this responsibility.

There is a (possibly apocryphal) story that explains why Germany have won so many penalty shootouts over the years. The story goes that in the days leading up to a knockout match, each player practices his own combination of three possible kicks. For example, the player might practice one kick bottom-left, one top-left, and one top-right. The player labels the kicks A, B and C.

When the game reaches a shootout, an especially tense and nerve-wracking situation that can cause players to freeze, the coach tells each of his five penalty takers which penalty option they will be kicking: A, B or C.

In that moment, the kicker is released from having to choose which direction to shoot, arguably his biggest stress and responsibility. If the keeper guesses correctly and saves, the player can reason that it was the coach's decision anyway. All the kicker needs to do is focus on making a clean contact and hitting the right area in the goal.

We can take that analogy and apply it to the relationship between the board and the manager. With the average managerial tenure well below 18 months in Europe's biggest leagues, it is clear that the manager bears the burden for poor results. This is largely because they often take responsibility for key decisions across different areas of the club, much in the same way non-German penalty takers must make a host of important choices before taking their kick.

But what if managers could be afforded some clarity of thought? Are there other people within the club who can take ownership of transfers, player management and succession planning? Fostering a sense of collective responsibility can relieve pressure and allow people to focus on their jobs.

Of course nothing is ever quite as straightforward as taking a penalty, but the principles of the German story apply: sharing the burden can often bring out the best results.

The Manager Surveillance System

It was Richard Fairbank, CEO of Capital One, who once said, "At most companies, people spend 2% of their time recruiting and 75% managing their recruiting mistakes".

The chances are your club will be hiring a new manager within the next twelve months. During the 2014/15 season, nearly 50% of clubs in the English Football League (47 of the 96) parted company with at least one manager.

So what can be done to increase the chances of making a successful managerial appointment?

When we advise clubs in this area we first look at context and urgency. Time and again we see clubs sack their manager after a bad run of results (often prematurely, when the underlying performance is actually on track), only to then commence the search process. Alternatively, a club might be left stranded as their incumbent manager is headhunted by a rival club. In such urgent moments it becomes a question of who is available, rather than who might be the right fit, and so the reactive cycle continues.

While it may sometimes feel like the situation is beyond a club's control, it is possible to be better prepared for these difficult moments. In the same way that clubs build succession plans for players, we've created a surveillance system for potential future managers. This horizon-scanning mechanism can identify certain traits that clubs should be looking for, including:

- Style: Does he play 'our way' (assuming the club has a defined philosophy)?

- Substance: What's his track record in terms of results and performance (the latter being a stronger indicator of future success)?

- Resourcefulness: Has he over or underachieved in previous roles relative to available resources?

In the corporate world, hiring for a position of equivalent influence can take a lot of time. Unfortunately for football clubs, time is not a luxury that many can afford. By applying relevant filters to a comprehensive manager database, clubs can keep tabs on prospective candidates that fit their desired criteria, enabling them to move decisively when the moment arrives.

This type of analysis doesn't negate the need for a thorough interview process of course. The manager surveillance system simply means that clubs can be more strategic about who they're interviewing, which in turn reduces the odds of being on the wrong side of the 50%.

Money Won't Buy a Legacy

It is common for national federations to speak of 'building a legacy', usually when bidding to host major tournaments or justifying their expense. Similar language has become more frequently used in club football of late, with teams mapping out legacy plans as they look to the future. As in the international game, it is generally thought that better facilities and spending increases can have a positive and lasting impact on a team's success and therefore constitute a 'legacy'.

However, by looking at the Elo ratings of countries that have hosted the World Cup and comparing the strength of those teams before and after their tournaments, only three nations – USA, Germany and Spain – can even begin to claim that hosting football's premier competition has led to sustained success.

In the case of the United States, it is indisputable that hosting the 1994 World Cup has had a lasting influence. For Germany and Spain, however, it is other, less tangible and more strategic changes that are the true heroes of their stories.

For all other World Cup hosts, the billions of dollars spent have resulted in national teams no better – and in many cases far worse – than the sides that took to the field in front of their home fans decades previously.

What can clubs learn from this? One lesson is that cosmetic changes, usually designed to please fans or attract sponsors, are often totally ineffectual in terms of building a legacy. This may seem obvious, but it bears repeating.

The national teams that have achieved genuine and sustained improvement in their on-field results have sought to set out clear strategic visions. Good examples of this include the Dutch side of the 1970s, and the current Belgian and Icelandic teams. New training grounds and commercial partnerships are nice, but they are rarely game-changers. Improvement comes from clear thinking and intelligent development work in key strategic areas.

Money won't buy a legacy. In many cases, it'll only buy a false dawn.

The Wages = Wins Fallacy

What if I told you that your wage bill is unrelated to your results?

It seems an absurd statement. In the Premier League, the correlation between wage bill and points across all teams is 82%. Although correlation does not mean causation, this figure is reasonably used to explain why less wealthy clubs will almost certainly finish below the likes of Manchester United and Chelsea each season.

However, while economics explains the gap in performance between the top and bottom teams, it struggles to explain the gaps within them.

If we divide the Premier League teams into 'rich' and 'poor' groups, suddenly there appears to be room for manoeuvre. Within the rich group, the correlation between how much you pay your players and where you finish in the league is 57%. Within the poor group, the correlation is just 38%. These are moderate relationships at best, particularly given the context.

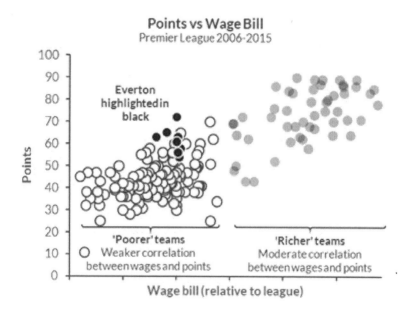

This means there are significant competitive advantages to be gained within each 'league within a league' given that each additional million spent on wages has an unpredictable relationship with position in the Premier League.

By benchmarking on-field success against your closest rivals instead of the entire league, there is greater opportunity to find competitive edge. Are the teams around you innovative or complacent? Do they react to results or make decisions based on underlying performance? Are they a club that nurtures or buys talent? Are they planning strategically for the future?

A lack of financial strength is often used as an excuse for failure, but there is actually more noise to the wages-wins relationship than we are led to believe. And where there is noise, there is opportunity.

Everton, by virtue of having been close to the median Premier League wage bill for a number of years, fall into the group of financially 'poor' clubs (compared to, for example, Chelsea, who have consistently been three times above the median). The Toffees won between 54 and 65 points each season from 2007 to 2013, while clubs with a similar wage bill averaged just 50 points during the same period. Clubs with a 15-25% bigger wage bill averaged even less at just 49 points. With astute leadership both on and off the field, Everton have found a competitive edge within their group and have even threatened to bridge the gap to the very richest teams.

It is impossible to deny that significant wealth gaps exist in every division, but it's more than possible to punch above your weight through smart decision-making without having to inflate the wage bill.

The Cost of Going Nowhere

Problem-solving in football has become synonymous with spending money.

If results aren't good enough, cheques are hastily signed for new players and coaching staff, with the cheaper and weaker replaced by those dearer and supposedly stronger. But how often is there a benefit to all this cost? Have teams that have gone through these processes tangibly improved, or simply gone in circles?

The Premier League is the wealthiest league in world football, but it has teams that are rich and poor relative to one another. Despite the commonly held belief that higher wages equal more wins, 21st Club's research has shown that the relationship pounds and point is vague at best.

Instead of comparing teams with their peer group, let's compare them with themselves. If, for example, a club moves from having the twelfth-highest wage bill to the eighth-highest from one season to the next, what is the impact on their results?

Change in points won vs change in wage bill
Premier League 2006-2015

The answer in the data is clear: the cost, on average, leaves you where you started.

The main exception to this rule is Manchester City. In the summer of 2009, the club made a quantum leap into the Premier League's richest group of teams following a bout of near-unprecedented spending. That newfound wealth led to an immediate return of 17 points on their investment.

For others however, the effect of increasing the wage bill relative to the league has had a range of both positive and negative effects. The reason for this non-relationship is simple. Without the luxury of being able to spend money on players who are clearly among the best in the world (as Manchester City and Chelsea have done), Premier League clubs have proved highly inefficient at identifying the difference, for example, between a £20,000 per week player and a £30,000 per week player. As such, luck plays a significant role in determining who gets real value from their wage bill, and who is left planning yet another squad overhaul.

Now consider the teams who have made notable step-changes in performance in recent seasons; Atlético Madrid, Borussia Mönchengladbach, Southampton and Saint-Étienne. Money may have played a part in their recent success, but it certainly hasn't been a magic bullet. Innovation in coaching, player recruitment and youth development have all played significant roles.

Sometimes problems can't be fixed with a credit card. Often, there's a cost to going nowhere.

What if the Way We Pay Our Players is Wrong?

Performance-related pay has become commonplace in football, with players typically incentivised to perform through individual and team targets. But how effective is this system? And does it really have a tangible effect on player behaviour?

Let's turn to a group of schoolchildren for some inspiration. In 2012, economist Steven Levitt and his colleagues decided to see if they could get students to perform better in tests by giving them cash rewards for improving on previous scores.

Perhaps unsurprisingly, students who were incentivised with money tended to make bigger improvements than those with no monetary incentive. Importantly, however, the incentive was more powerful when it was framed as a loss.

The authors compared two groups of students: those who were given money after the test only if they met their performance standard (much like the model in football today), and those who were given money before the test and had it taken away if they failed to meet the required scores. Fuelled by the fear of losing money, the second group tended to make more significant improvements than the first. The students in the second group tried harder than those attempting to win the cash. In other words, the pain from a potential loss outweighed the pleasure from a potential gain.

Is it possible that footballers could react in the same way? If players were paid a monthly salary that included bonuses, having money deducted for not achieving certain performance targets, would it change their behaviour?

Picture a team that is 2-0 down after 60 minutes. Under a normal incentive scheme, the players may have already resigned themselves to missing out on a win bonus. Whether conscious or unconscious, their commitment may fade in the knowledge that they will be no worse off financially after the game. Under the 'schoolchildren' performance incentive, might the players work harder to avoid defeat given the prospect of a loss of earnings coming their way?

The timing of the payout may also be important, as the authors of the school study highlight. A bonus paid out at the end of the season may feel more like a reward than an incentive; a retrospective gift to recognise hard work, rather than a target that could influence behaviour during the season. Recognising performance achievements during the season could more effectively encourage players to deliver when it counts.

The practicality of changing the current performance pay system in football would need careful thought, as it is vital that the players clearly understand and respect the club's bonus policy. However, it is always useful to challenge the status quo and, in this case, question the way players are rewarded.

40

II: TALENT

What if the Answer Lies in the Room?

Football is full of blind spots that can affect our decision making: the short-term view that can't see the long-term view; the football view that can't see the financial view; the player we want versus the player we've already got. The list goes on.

The final few days of the transfer window only serve to exacerbate how blinkered our view is. The problem is not a deliberate desire to be unfair, but rather our inability to view information objectively given the intensity created by a closing window of opportunity.

Whatever your circumstance, the transfer window represents a chance to freshen up your squad. For clubs with a long-term focus, the opportunity is to invest in the future by signing young players whose value could rise as they mature into peak performance. For others, the short-term is the priority, which invariably means paying a premium for quick fix solutions to unexpected problems.

The situation and context will be different at each club, although we should always challenge potential player acquisitions in the same way. Some questions worth asking include:

- Does the player align with our club's philosophy and fit with our style of play?

- How have other last-minute signings performed historically, both for us and for other clubs?

- How long did other similar players take to adapt?

- Which type of players have previously transitioned faster than others?

- Do we have any data to give us an objective assessment of player performance?

- Do we already have a player with the similar profile at the club, whether they be on the fringes of the first team or even in the academy?

Southampton's recent success in the Premier League would suggest that there is merit in looking within the club for a fresh injection of talent. During the 2013/14 season, Southampton brought in just three new faces as they promoted four youngsters to the first team squad and continued to rely on the core players from the previous campaign. The squad enjoyed a similar level of stability in 2012/13 as the club avoided relegation during its first season back in the Premier League.

In life it's natural to desire things we don't have. Managers understandably want to bring in tried and tested players rather than promoting a less experienced talent from within, given the pressure to deliver immediate success. But there's a contradiction here, in that many managers often express the concern that new players need more time to settle in.

In a world of Financial Fair Play and the Elite Player Performance Plan, where there is pressure to bring in new faces during the transfer window, it's at least worth asking the question: what if the answer lies in the room?

Player Recruitment: Why One Size Doesn't Fit All

In November 2014, former England midfielder Paul Scholes criticised the organisational structure of some football clubs, putting forward the view that managers should be in charge of signing players.

Scholes' column can be paraphrased as follows:

1. A director of football at a club is under pressure.

2. The director of football plays an important role in player recruitment, but doesn't have to manage the players on a daily basis.

3. The club's signings have not met expectations in the last 18 months.

4. At Manchester United, Sir Alex Ferguson was in charge of player recruitment.

5. Ferguson had huge success over many years.

6. A manager's future is dependent on the team's results, so he should be in charge of signing the players he has to manage.

7. Directors of football are symptomatic of overstaffing at football clubs.

8. Clubs could save money by cutting staff and leaving player recruitment calls to a smaller pool of people.

It's an interesting point, except of course it's possible to make the exact opposite argument using very similar themes:

1. A manager at a club is under pressure.

2. He plays an important role in player recruitment, but must focus on short-term results to keep his job.

3. The club's signings have not met expectations in the last 18 months.

4. West Bromwich Albion have for many years employed technical directors who are responsible for overseeing player recruitment.

5. The club has stayed in the Premier League against all odds.

6. A club's future is dependent on building sustainable success, so should be focused on buying players for the long term.

7. Many managers are overworked and at least 50% of new signings are underutilised.

8. Clubs could save money by reducing recruitment mistakes.

Both arguments are one-sided and use anecdotes to generalise about complex issues.

The Ferguson model may not work everywhere because not all managers have the job security to pursue both individual and club objectives. The director of football model may not work everywhere because some clubs are better served by leveraging their manager's pulling power. In a number of cases, joined-up thinking between a few key parties may work best.

The point is this: there is no one size fits all process for player recruitment. Establish what is important to your club, align objectives, and build a structure that enables you to meet your goals.

Make Three Rules

Imagine, for a moment, that you wanted to make three rules for the transfer window by which your club must abide.

After some thought, you set out these simple guidelines for new signings:

1. Signings must be 25 years old or younger, so we get their peak years.

2. Signings must have played more than 70% of available minutes last season, so we know they've been consistently fit and selected.

3. Signings must be bought from teams at least as good as ours.

You could visualise the qualifying players in a Venn diagram. For example, a selection of signings made by Premier League teams in 2015/16:

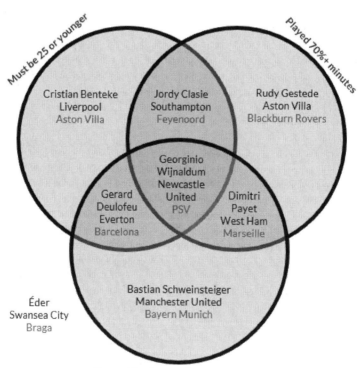

As a club, you might decide that these rules are just a guideline, or that you only need to abide by one. Perhaps you have different rules altogether, depending on the situation at your club. It might be that if one of the rules is not met, a player would have to score highly on the other two metrics to make your shortlist.

Arguably more important is keeping track of what happens to players who meet or miss these rules. How many of our signings that met rules one and two, but missed three, for example, went on to become quantifiable successes? What about the players who comfortably met all three?

Recruitment is not an exact science, but it needn't be a crapshoot either. Defining a basic recruitment philosophy and holding ourselves to account can help us to outsmart the opposition in the transfer market and achieve a level of competitive advantage.

Seven Days of Deals, Four Types of Club

The overlapping of the final weeks of the transfer window and the start of the domestic season can be an awkward time for clubs. Some would prefer to focus on extracting the best from their existing squad, while others are drawn into player trading by the opportunities offered by the window.

As long as the window exists, we will always have four different types of clubs behaving in different ways as deadline day approaches:

> 1. Overachieved and active: clubs that have enjoyed good results early in the season, with three or more players brought in (either bought or loaned) during the final week of the window.

> 2. Overachieved and inactive: these are clubs with good early season results, but little incoming transfer activity during as the window draws to a close.

> 3. Underachieved and inactive: clubs that have produced below-par results early on in the season, but have brought in very few players during the final week.

> 4. Underachieved and active: below-par early results coupled with players bought or loaned during the final week.

Each point on the chart represent a Premier League or Championship club's incoming transfer activity during the final week of the window, plotted against the level of over or underachievement in results at time of deadline day (achievement being calculated by looking at actual results against bookmakers' odds).

Not all clubs we analysed were necessarily reacting to their results. Some deals take many weeks to close, and occasional opportunism during this period should not be seen as a negative trait. For those that did react though, it's important to remember that early season results generally have a weak relationship with a club's final points tally. Clubs should instead look to more meaningful signals, such as the team's underlying performance, which can be measured and has been shown to have a strong correlation with long-term patterns of results.

Final week signings vs pre-deadline over/underachievement
Premier League & Championship 2010-2014

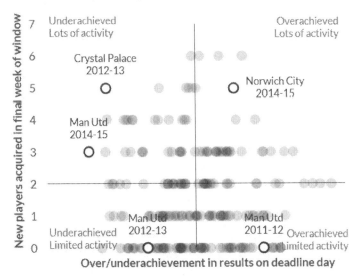

One club that has historically been inactive during the final week of the window is Manchester United. In Sir Alex Ferguson's last three seasons at the club, they did not bring in a single new player during that period, irrespective of how results had gone. Circumstances have since changed, however, as signalled by the arrivals of Radamel Falcao, Angel Di Maria and Daley Blind in the final week of the 2014 summer window during a particularly poor run of results.

As the summer window draws to a close, it can be difficult to know exactly what to expect before January. However, it's always worth asking what type of club you want as one window closes and you make preparations for the winter.

For Every Talented Player

For every talented player...

There is an agent telling stories about the player's skill and future potential.

There are multiple scouts watching every performance, scribbling down notes.

There are 150 scouts sat at training grounds trawling through reports.

There are 500 sporting directors and technical analysts watching video and making clips.

The world is now flat. Footage is accessible online. Data has become ubiquitous. In this environment, we need to ask ourselves an important question: what are we are doing differently to gain a competitive edge in the transfer market?

Everything else is just the same.

An Alternative to Agents

Agents have a bad reputation in football, the common perception being that they only have their own financial interests at heart, unsettling players wherever possible and using the media to engineer deals. They then leverage their relationships to play various clubs off against each other, making exorbitant commission fees in the process and draining much-needed money from the game. Ergo, football agents are the scourge of modern day football.

Agents fees continue to rise, not that that surprises anyone. Transfer fees (up 29% in 2014) and player wages (up 10% in 2013) are also on the rise, fuelled by highly lucrative broadcast deals. Agents' commissions have risen proportionally, going hand-in-hand with inflation in the game. However, agents are as much the effect as they are the cause.

The better intermediaries can justifiably claim to serve an important function. With only two windows of opportunity available for player trading, agents should act as a means of expediting the movement of talent between clubs. In theory, this should help the market to achieve greater levels of efficiency, although we know it doesn't always play out that way.

Over time, technology could serve to diminish the influence of agents. FIFA's Global Player Exchange (GPX), for example, looks to streamline the player trading process by offering new channels of communication between clubs. However, the use of technology is only really a means of achieving greater efficiency, accelerating rather than a triggering change. It may be that technology simply replaces agents as the middle man without truly altering the system.

The only real alternative to agents is for clubs to change their focus from player trading to player development, making a long-term commitment to cultivating young talent through the academy system. In the future, the more strategic and courageous clubs will have very little need for agents at all.

The Overrated Factor

In the final weeks of the transfer window, boardrooms are increasingly required to make quick decisions under pressure.

In this environment, we often try to evaluate complex choices by relying on small and simple pieces of information. This can be useful in some cases, but often such information is misunderstood.

Take 'having experience', for example. In the English Championship, received wisdom would have us believe that a squad full of players with experience in the division is a good thing. The reasoning is simple: the season is long and physical, and it can be a shock to the uninitiated.

However, when you control for the cost of a squad, there is no relationship between amount of experience and final league position. Experience is overvalued by received wisdom.

Points won vs Championship experience
Bubble size is squad wage bill

The cases of Southampton and Leicester City during the 2011/12 season are illustrative. Southampton, newly promoted from League One, had just a handful of players with recent Championship experience but comfortably achieved promotion to the Premier League. Leicester City's squad, meanwhile, had plenty of experience in the division, but failed to make a serious push for a play-off spot. There are countless other examples of teams with similar wage bills but different experience profiles finishing well above or below one another.

It's true that good Championship teams will often – but not always – have experience in the division, but that is not what makes them effective. Teams that have squads of similar cost but less divisional experience do just as well. This may present an opportunity for smart clubs to find undervalued players in the market.

Experience is just one of the factors we might overrate under pressure. Is it important that a player has international caps, or has never been relegated? Can we put a value on the fact he seems 'down to earth'?

A clear process, supported with data where possible, can enable us to make better-informed decisions and avoid overpaying, particularly in the final days of the window.

The Next Jamie Vardy

Jamie Vardy's record run of 11 goals in 11 consecutive Premier League matches in 2015/16 was a remarkable feat. The record was made all the more astonishing by the fact that Vardy was playing in England's seventh tier just four and a half years previously.

Vardy's journey from the lower leagues to the national team has got clubs and the media wondering where the next Jamie Vardy might be found. Vardy's story makes us want to believe that there are more of these undiscovered talents out there, but the uniqueness of his situation should really tell us that the odds of finding such a player are very small. Just 17 Premier League players in 2015/16 had played non-league football, and none but Vardy were still playing at that level at the age of 22. What's more, the odds of success widen further when countless other clubs are in search of the same 'diamond in the rough'.

Vardy is an exception. By the age of 24 virtually all players are playing at a level close to which they will peak. It is possible to build a player recruitment strategy around finding exceptions, but given limited data this approach is likely to produce high failure rates. It is essentially squad planning roulette.

Without the resources or data to search far and wide, there are ways to go about player recruitment more systematically, by identifying the traits and trends that typically point to success. By identifying the characteristics of our most successful and unsuccessful signings, recruitment policies can be devised by isolating and rectifying problems in the search and due diligence processes.

Vardy's success should be celebrated, but it certainly wasn't predicted. A recruitment strategy with no means by which to forecast success simply isn't sustainable.

How Much Should We Pay?

In the closing weeks of the football season, attention inevitably turns to the summer and the impending transfer window. Bogus media speculation will clog the back pages, while fans will take to social media in an effort to encourage their teams to spend big on new players.

At the centre of the melee will be clubs, all attempting to negotiate a path littered with obstacles and inconsistencies. It is no wonder that transfer deals and player contracts are threaded with complexity.

So how can clubs best prepare for the challenges that they are faced with each summer? One method is to establish a budget for each transfer target based on the role they are expected to fulfil. This can be done through establishing how much a first team minute is worth to the club.

Let's imagine that we are a Premier League club with a total wage bill of £62.5m, of which around 60% is apportioned to the first team. Given that there are 37,620 available first team minutes over the course of a league campaign (11 players, 38 games of 90 minutes each), we can estimate that the value of one minute is roughly £1,000.

We can use this basic calculation to apply budget thresholds to some hypothetical case studies:

Transfer target	Squad role allocation	Expected utilisation	Expected utilisation (minutes)	Low weekly wage threshold	High weekly wage threshold
Peak age player bought to make an immediate impact on the first team	Core player	50 - 100%	1,710 - 3,420	£33k	£66k
Pre-peak age player bought to develop at the club	Squad player	20 - 50%	684 - 1,710	£13k	£33k
Post-peak age player bought for squad depth and experience	Fringe player	0 - 20%	0 - 684	£0k	£13k

Clearly, this is not perfect solution. You can't expect to pay a fringe player nothing just because he might not play. There are other ways that players can add value to a club outside of playing which carry a monetary value; leadership skills, for example. Furthermore, clubs may be willing to 'overpay' to sign a marquee name, while the market also assigns different values by position.

Although simplistic, this sort of calculation does give us a useful starting point by providing rational, objective grounding for any negotiation, while forcing clubs to carefully consider the roles that transfer targets are expected to fulfil. It would also require clubs to proactively justify wage demands that fall outside of these thresholds.

Given the challenges that lie in wait each summer, having a logical, objective baseline for negotiation enables a more rational process and may just help your club stick to its strategic plans.

Signs of Success

The success of new signings is often described in intangible or individualistic terms. For example, we might hear that a new centre back "added leadership" in defence, or that a new striker "scored 7 in 12". There is nothing wrong with these assessments per se, but too often there is no truly objective evaluation of a player's impact on team performance.

One way of doing this is to look at a prediction model as it stands today. In the English Championship in January 2016, the average prediction of 21st Club's model had Derby County winning around 84 points by the end of the season. This prediction was based on past performance and remaining fixtures; all information acquired before the January transfer window.

Team	On 21st January		Expected End of Season	
	Position	Points	Position	Points
Middlesbrough	1	55	1	91.6
Hull City	2	53	2	86.8
Derby County	3	49	3	84.0
Burnley	4	48	4	77.5
Brighton and Hove Albion	5	47	5	77.0
Ipswich Town	7	45	6	73.8
Sheffield Wednesday	6	45	7	72.0
Birmingham City	8	43	8	67.9
Cardiff City	9	40	9	65.4
Wolverhampton Wanderers	10	37	10	64.6
Brentford	11	36	11	62.6
Reading	14	34	12	62.6
Queens Park Rangers	15	34	13	60.4
Preston North End	13	35	14	60.4
Nottingham Forest	12	35	15	60.4
Blackburn Rovers	18	29	16	56.9
Leeds United	17	32	17	55.7
Huddersfield Town	16	32	18	54.6
Fulham	19	28	19	49.8
Bristol City	22	24	20	48.7
MK Dons	20	26	21	45.6
Rotherham United	21	24	22	44.7
Charlton Athletic	23	20	23	37.6
Bolton Wanderers	24	17	24	37.0

If Derby's transfer activity that winter had been an immediate success, it would have been reasonable to expect that the club would have exceeded that 84-point expectation. The same would apply to clubs in any other league. Of course, exceeding (or failing to meet) such expectations can come down to any number of factors including luck, tactical changes, players returning from injury and so on, but the prediction serves as a benchmark and is a useful starting point for discussion.

At your own club, clarifying how many points you expect your new signings to add can be a useful exercise, creating a second benchmark and point of accountability.

The transfer window is sometimes seen as a one stop shop for solutions to a club's problems. This objective approach to expectation benchmarking offers some clarity on how much of a solution the window really provides.

An Avoidable Distraction

September always brings a certain tranquility to football as the annual melee of deadline day is left behind. As the clock runs down on August, buying clubs rush to bolster their squad, while selling clubs look to offload their expensive, unproductive assets. Indeed, since 2010 a sizeable 18% of business in the Premier League has been conducted during the last week of the window.

This reveals much about the nature of football; planning is hard, competition is fierce and circumstance often dictates a requirement to act late. However, the extent of activity during the latter stages of the window suggests that choice does play a part in continuing to trade right up until the deadline.

But by the time the window closes, 8% of Premier League games have already been completed, rising to 10% in the Football League. This may not sound like much, but for clubs who might later be on the cusp of relegation or Champions League qualification, it can mean the difference between success or failure.

This is especially true of clubs whose early fixtures are against rivals in a similar context to themselves. Take Middlesbrough in 2016/17, for example. Their opening fixtures against Stoke City, Sunderland and West Bromwich Albion were not only opportunities to enhance their own prospects, but also to dent those of their rivals. Those games were therefore crucially important to the club's quest to stay in the Premier League, even at such an early stage of the season.

We can better understand this by assessing the number of points expected from the first three matches as a percentage of projected end-of-season points based on the bookmaker's spreads. This is calculated using 21st Club's statistical models and objectively comparing the relative strengths and weaknesses of the teams.

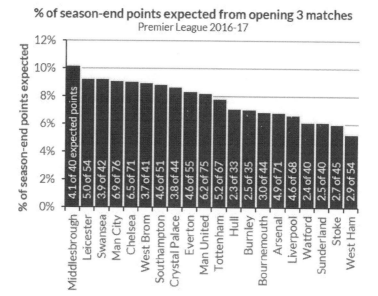

% of season-end points expected from opening 3 matches
Premier League 2016-17

% of season-end points expected

Bar values (left to right):
- Middlesbrough — 4.1 of 40 expected points
- Leicester — 5.0 of 54
- Swansea — 3.9 of 42
- Man City — 6.9 of 76
- Chelsea — 6.5 of 71
- West Brom — 3.7 of 41
- Southampton — 4.6 of 51
- Crystal Palace — 3.8 of 44
- Everton — 4.6 of 55
- Man United — 6.2 of 75
- Tottenham — 5.2 of 67
- Hull — 2.3 of 33
- Burnley — 2.5 of 35
- Bournemouth — 3.0 of 44
- Arsenal — 4.9 of 71
- Liverpool — 4.6 of 68
- Watford — 2.4 of 40
- Sunderland — 2.5 of 40
- Stoke — 2.7 of 45
- West Ham — 2.9 of 54

According to this metric, the first three games of the 2016/17 season were more important for Middlesbrough than any other team in the Premier League. In fact, Boro were expected to win 10% of their season's points total in the first three games of the season.

Securing key signings early on, as well as avoiding the unsettling impact that extensive transfer speculation can have on the team, was key to improving the club's chances of accruing valuable early points. Therefore, it is likely to have been satisfying for the club to see Álvaro Negredo – the club's star loan signing who joined early in the window – featuring prominently in their strong start to the season.

Amid the excitement of signing players, it is easy to forget that points won in August are just as valuable as those won later on in the season. The distraction of signing a raft of last minute stars may just come at a price that can only be quantified once the season draws to a close.

Predicting Your Future Squad

Meet Gavin. Gavin is 17 years old and has just signed a professional contract at a top Premier League club. He's played for England at an under-17 World Cup, and is already warming the bench for the first team in the League Cup.

What are the chances of Gavin becoming an established first team player for his club? You might think they're quite high, based off the limited information above. Indeed, in 2007 one newspaper tipped Gavin – Hoyte, of Arsenal – as a potential starter at the 2014 World Cup. Of course, this prediction turned out to be wildly off the mark.

It is easy to mock these predictions, but they reflect the inherent difficulties in forecasting the futures of our young players. Indeed, it is often hard to predict what our squad will look like next season, let alone four, five or six years down the line.

But here's a little exercise for you to try.

Get a list of every U21, academy or youth player in your club. Next to each name, mark the probability (on a scale of 0-1) that, at some point in the next six years, the player will at least be a semi-regular member of the first team.

For your standout under-21 players, it may be that you give them a 50-75% chance. For younger players it may be best to assign them a base rate in line with the proportion of under-18 players that have made it through to your first team in the last 10 years. This might be around 5%, and so translates to a 0.05 chance.

Next, dust off the calculator and add up the probabilities you've assigned to each player. If you have, for example, 20 players at 20% (0.2) and 10 players at 50% (0.5), the numbers will add up to nine. This means you would expect nine players to reach the first team within the next six years. This figure becomes a starting point for evaluating return on investment in youth development. Would nine players (or whatever your number is) be an acceptable target given your costs? Secondly, the number acts as a benchmark to which everyone at the club is accountable and can work towards.

Six years may seem like a long time in football, but they are crucial years for the development of our young players. Do your current plans create blockages in their pathways to the first team? How would sending these players out on loan affect their chances? In which positions are you likely to have holes in the squad, based on your estimates?

Prediction is rarely about whether a player definitely will or won't make it; individual situations are generally shades of grey, reflecting the uncertainty of talent and opportunity. We're dealing with human beings after all. This probabilistic approach is both risk savvy and creates more reasonable expectations when talking to a player about his future. It may also save the club from pinning its hopes on one or two of its very own Gavins.

Knowledge: The Antidote to Fear in Player Development

The Guardian's Sean Ingle wrote an article in February 2015 questioning whether England was on the verge of producing another 'Golden Generation' of footballers in light of the form of players such as Harry Kane, Dele Alli and Jordon Ibe. As part of his piece, Ingle noted a remarkable drop in the number of players starting in Premier League first teams who were under the age of 24:

In the early 70s and 80s, between 35% and 37% of starting appearances in the old Division One were made by footballers [under the age of 24]. *Despite the FA's Blueprint for Football promising in 1991 that the Premier League would emphasise developing English talent, those numbers have continued to slide. In 2011-2012 just 21% of top-flight starters were 23 or younger. This season* [2014/15] *it is 17.4% – the lowest in the modern era.*

This, despite increased investment in youth academies and younger player development.

It is reasonable to suggest that there are a few powerful trends responsible for this drop. Chief among them is surely the influx of ever greater television revenues into the Premier League, money that has significantly raised the stakes for top flight clubs desperate to stay up every year. This—coupled with the continued dual roles of the football manager, who is often both coach and player recruiter in chief—has led to a situation in which an individual in a very vulnerable, public position has a tremendous amount of cash available to buy a first eleven that will not only have to keep the club afloat, but keep them in a job a little longer. I don't think all of this is a conscious development, but simply the result of a number of factors outside any one person's control.

One obvious solution would be to give more power over recruitment to the technical director, a person generally kept out of the media spotlight whose job security extends beyond a few short-term results. It may be even more helpful to address the root cause of the failure of English clubs to start more of their young players:

Fear.

How do we counter fear? With knowledge. How certain are we that this lightning quick, razor sharp 22-year-old winger in the reserves won't suddenly crash and burn when they join the first team? How many games can the club risk on this player before we know whether or not they will develop into a bona fide star?

Developing reliable predictive metrics is one way, but the continued development of analytics is providing clubs with more ways to measure the unseen ways a player may contribute to a winning performance. This information could one day help youth academy staff to better work with their players to both help them reach their full potential, and to provide first team staff with more reliable knowledge about their younger players, removing some of the fear associated with starting them.

It's important to note here that there are already several European clubs who rely on their youth products not out of choice, but financial necessity. They don't exist in leagues with TV deals that would allow them to buy a first team wholesale, and they rely on transfer fees for finished products as a revenue source. Some teams have perfected this process more than others, but the important thing to note is that the most successful among them trust their youth systems because it has worked in the past. The fear-cancelling knowledge doesn't reside in the individual players, but the system itself.

A reinvestment of some of that TV money into a smarter, more comprehensive approach to team management and player development won't just help the individual club, but national football development as a whole.

The Cost of Sidelined Talent

The final weeks of a domestic season see us begin to reflect on where it has gone right or wrong for our teams. What changes could we have made and where were we unlucky?

Whenever we think about luck in football, discussion of injuries is never far away. Whilst not without reason, at many levels the occurrence of an injury is random and unprejudiced towards geography or talent. Teams can simply be unlucky if they have more key players out than their rivals.

Clubs are also not in control of the strength of their opponents. In some weeks they may face an opposition without its most valuable players, while others they may take on a team at full strength.

In a league with fine margins, these factors can make a difference. Using data from the 2014/15 Premier League season, 21st Club has plotted the average proportion of squad value injured of one's own team against the average of the opposition on the day of each game.

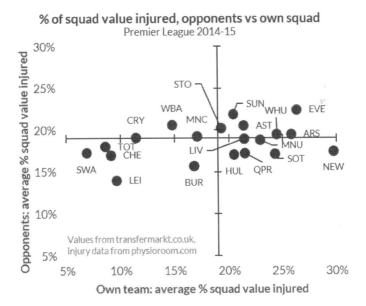

% of squad value injured, opponents vs own squad
Premier League 2014-15

Using player value, rather than a simple count, means that an injury to a more important player has more weight than an injury to a young prospect or fringe player. Everton, for example, suffered a number of injuries to valuable individuals throughout the 2014/15 campaign, but also encountered opponents with similar issues on several occasions.

In the opposing quadrant, Leicester City had relatively few high-value players sidelined, but also faced opponents with few costly injuries. Fellow relegation strugglers Burnley, Hull and QPR also encountered an above-average number of games where the opposition was near full strength, while all suffering costlier injuries than Leicester. By no means does this fully explain those clubs' league positions, but it does add context to match results.

It may be impossible to consider and control for all the factors that influence the look of the league table, but data can help with future contingency planning. With an effective succession plan in place, clubs can be ready to bring younger talent into the first team when injuries inevitably occur.

Counting the Cost of the International Break

For Premier League and Championship clubs, the September international break is the football equivalent of adverts just ten minutes into a TV programme. At the very moment the season is kicking into gear, its momentum is disrupted and we're not always sure if we'll like what we see on the other side.

Players either return having enjoyed some time off, or in varying states of fitness after travelling on international duty. In the brief time before the next round of games, clubs are often left literally counting the cost of injuries within the squad, given some absences are more damaging than others.

Instead of merely counting the number of players each Premier League team had injured in September 2014, we have assessed the expense of individual injuries as a proportion of the squad's total value, broken down by comparing those sustained before and during the international break.

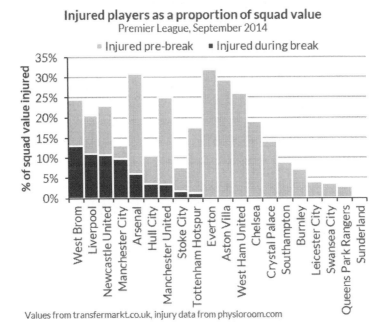

Injured players as a proportion of squad value
Premier League, September 2014

Values from transfermarkt.co.uk, injury data from physioroom.com

Whilst publicly accessible injury data is imperfect, this analysis at least gives us an estimate for the cost of the international break to the clubs of the Premier League (recognising that not all injuries during the break were sustained by players on international duty).

In September 2014, the average Premier League team had 16% of the value of its squad out injured. Unfortunately for West Bromwich Albion, 13% of their squad value picked up injuries during the break to add to the 11% already out. Some clubs – including Everton, Aston Villa and West Ham – had players with pre-existing injuries and would have been glad that the situation did not deteriorate ahead of upcoming fixtures.

In a post-World Cup season like 2014/15, injuries can come both as one-off incidents and as an accumulation of fatigue, so it would be foolish and unconstructive to assign blame for absences. Equally, international breaks can provide a chance for already-injured players to recover and return to fitness.

Nevertheless, given the opportunity to regroup before the next flurry of games, assigning a financial value to squad availability can enable clubs to gain a fuller perspective on the status of the first team. Reacting to a simple tally of injured players can lead to clouded decision-making. Tracking the value-availability of players over time is a more robust way of measuring the impact of your sidelined talent.

The Fringe Player Dilemma

It's easy to forget about your fringe players. When your season largely rests upon the actions of 15 to 18 key individuals, you can quickly lose focus around the purpose of the rest of the squad. We all recognise that squads need depth, but what type of profile is required for your backup players?

By grouping players as 'core', 'squad' and 'fringe', the characteristics of a squad become measurable and comparable. According to our analysis, in a typical squad the 10 most frequently appearing outfielders each play more than 50% of available minutes during a season. They are your core players, and, if available, the first names on the team sheet. The next seven squad players each play on average between 20% and 50% of minutes, whilst fringe players each tend to play less than 20% of minutes.

By chance or design, different clubs have different compositions of fringe players. Some will favour youth, occasionally providing opportunities in the first team as part of the club's succession plan. Others will opt for more experience in the hope that those players can provide leadership in the dressing room. During the 2013/14 Premier League season, just one of seven (14%) of Tottenham's fringe players were over the age of 23, whilst all six of Hull's backups were in the peak or roll-down phases of their careers.

In the 2013/14 Championship campaign, Sheffield Wednesday stood out as a team that mixed an experienced core with younger fringe players, whilst teams like Blackburn and Leicester generally opted for old heads in reserve, especially when compared to their core and squad players.

Notwithstanding the benefits of having experienced players around the dressing room, the issue with carrying a high number of over-23s in the fringes of the squad is twofold: they can become high cost/low productivity passengers, and they arguably block the pathway for younger talent. When margins are fine, it's vital to get the composition of the squad right year-on-year.

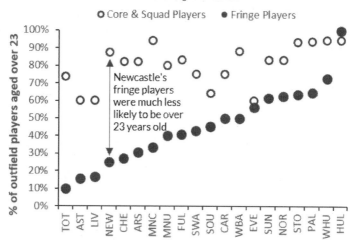

% of outfield players aged over 23 years old, by squad status
Premier League 2013-14

All of this should make you ask yourself whether your fringe players are serving the right purpose. If not, what is the evolution plan for next season?

The 20th Player

In 1984, Liverpool famously used just 15 outfield players in a 66-game season. 12 of those individuals played in over half of those matches, with just three fringe players providing cover.

Football has changed dramatically during the intervening three decades. Large squads are now the norm and rotation is an accepted part of the game. However, teams still generally rely on a 'core' group of 10 outfield players playing over 50% of available minutes, while the 15th most-appearing player plays an average of around 25% of minutes.

Minutes played by nth-most appearing outfield player
Selected leagues, averages

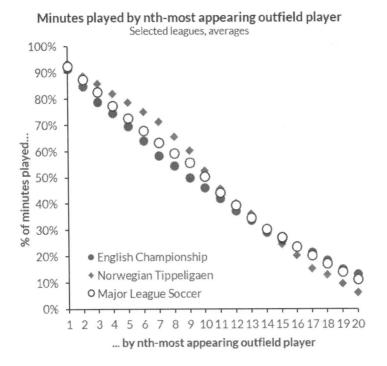

... by nth-most appearing outfield player

But what of the 20th player? What kind of individual do we want in this role? Virtually all teams use at least 20 outfield players in a season, and on average this player features in around 10% of possible minutes (nine minutes per game). In Norway this figure drops as low as 6%, and is as high as 13% in the English Championship.

Should the 20th player be a veteran to whom the manager can turn in high-pressure situations? Or are clubs better served by having a youngster in that role, an individual who is not a core player today but must start somewhere?

A quick scan of the data tells us that players like Aaron Ramsey (when aged 17), Daniel Sturridge (20) and Mario Götze (17) have all been the 20th most-appearing player at specific times in their careers. Indeed, most young players will have started somewhere around 20th in the pecking order, with a view to rising up the ranks year-by-year.

Nine minutes per game may not seem like much, but accumulated over a season it can represent crucial experience for a young player and may ultimately benefit the club in the long run. It's not always easy to give an unknown quantity a chance, but the 20th player might be a good place to start.

Heads or Tails?

It's natural in life to want new things, but given football's proclivity for expensive transfer dealings, I wanted to know how many new signings actually turn out to be an immediate success.

"Less than half" was the prompt response from one of the analysts in our offIce, having quickly queried the database. He had run a search on the percentage of possible minutes played by new signings and found that only 40% played more than half of the available first team minutes in their first season (for context, 'core' players in a squad typically play between 50 and 100% of first team minutes according to our research, so that's the benchmark for success given that the purpose of making new signings is to improve the team).

Granted, some clubs bring in young talent as a long-term investment for the future, or more experienced players as backup. However, even when you control for this by looking at 24-30 year olds, the new players signed with the intention of making an immediate impact still only played 48% of minutes.

In short: the chance of a new signing being successful essentially boils down to a coin toss.

Recruitment is hard, but in football we should arguably be better at finding new talent than other industries. Why? Because we are able to watch potential new hires perform (traditional scouting) and we have remote access to data and video to help us make our decisions.

There is no silver bullet. Often it's simply about shifting the odds in your favour through adopting smart approaches and deciding who *not* to buy.

The £999,999 Problem

What time do you set your alarm in the morning? The odds are it's a round number; 6:30am rather than 6:27am, for example.

This simple decision is relatively inconsequential, as a minute here or there isn't going to make you late for work. However, analysis of historical football transfers suggests that round numbers can play an important role in influencing some of the game's biggest decisions.

To provide an insight into the significance of numbers in decision-making, we've summarised the 100 most expensive transfers of all time by the age of the player when he was bought. The majority of players in this subset were bought between the ages of 23 and 27, with a reasonable proportion either side of that age group.

A curious thing happens when a player hits 30, however. 10 of the most expensive signings of all time have been players aged 28 or 29, but only one player in this subset was bought after his 30th birthday (the 31-year-old Gabriel Batistuta in 2000). This is a severe drop-off, no doubt influenced by the fact that it is much easier to convince ourselves of the value of a deal when a key characteristic falls just below a significant number.

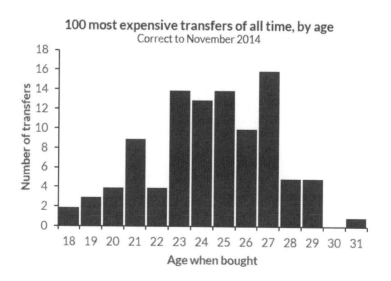

100 most expensive transfers of all time, by age
Correct to November 2014

Previous 21st Club analysis has suggested that, rationally speaking, this drop-off should come around the ages of 26 or 27. Whilst there is some evidence that clubs broadly obey this rule, it's a round number, 30, that has a powerful role in these decisions. The signings of some high-profile 29-year-olds, including Andriy Shevchenko and Robin van Persie, were arguably perceived to be disproportionately more justifiable given they were the right side of 30.

Similarly, batters in baseball are known to behave very differently when performing just below a .300 average, as compared to those just on or above that mystical round number. There is a notable difference in the financial rewards offered by teams for otherwise comparable players, too.

You may be asking what record-breaking transfers and baseball statistics have to do with you. The reason is simple: December and January are a time of key decisions, both in the transfer window and contract renegotiations. It is therefore worth thinking whether you would be planning to spend as much money on new players if your club was just outside the relegation zone, rather than just inside it? Would the new salary offered to a star player be as high if he had scored 19 goals rather than 20? Is a player perceived to be of lower value because his salary is £9,900 a week, rather than £10,000?

Round numbers may bring comfort and understanding, but at busy times of year they can act as the tiny bacteria that turn an entire process rotten. Objective decision making is hard and made even harder when we are in competition with our own biases.

Sunk Cost Bias

Concorde was an incredible feat of aeronautical engineering. First flown in 1969, the supersonic airliner entered service in 1976, making it possible to fly from London to New York in as little as two hours, fifty-two minutes (and fifty-nine seconds, to be precise).

However, Concorde also proved to be an enormous financial failure, losing money for more than four decades. Yet each time it went over budget the French and British governments poured more and more money into the project, despite knowing that they had no chance of recouping their continued investment.

According to Greg McKeown in his best-selling book *Essentialism: The Disciplined Pursuit of Less*, sunk cost bias is the tendency to continue to invest time, money and energy into something we know is a losing proposition. We do this simply because we have already incurred, or sunk, a cost that cannot be recouped.

In a football context, sunk cost bias is apparent when an expensive signing doesn't work out and we find it hard to let go (often for a fraction of the initial deal). The more we invest, the harder it is to let go as we become paralysed by our determination to make it work, or the embarrassment at having made a poor decision. We may also experience similar feelings when academy talents don't make it through to the first team, despite having spent years nurturing them through the system.

In reality, previous outlay (like how much you spent on a player) has nothing to do with future economic outcomes (like what that player is worth today). That's tough to accept, but it's true.

A good way to decide whether it's time to cut your losses is to ask yourself a simple question: If I could go back in time and sign that player again, would I?

The Journey of a Successful Team

The chart below tracks the age profile of a well-known team over three periods between 1998 and 2014. Which period do you think produced the most success?

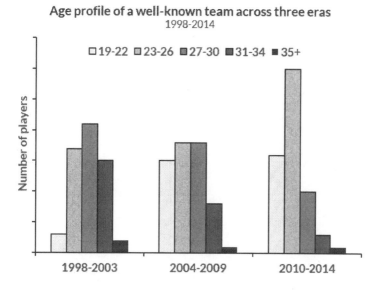

Age profile of a well-known team across three eras
1998-2014

On limited information there's no obvious answer, but first impressions might go as follows:

- 1998-2003: plenty of peak-age players combined with experience.

- 2004-2009: a balance of ages across the squad, with some young players coming through.

- 2010-2014: a reliance on young players with limited experience in support.

Despite an apparent lack of experience, this team enjoyed its most successful years between 2010 and 2014. Just over a decade before, between 1998 and 2003, its fans had lost their passion for the team, disillusioned with mediocre performances in big matches.

In its most recent era, the team was able to compensate for a lack of older players by developing players smarter and more talented than their predecessors, and were brave enough to give these talents a chance. A succession plan was put in place and the team reaped the rewards as players were steadily absorbed into the first team to gain experience. Success soon followed.

The team, of course, is Germany. Germany's story is well-known but bears repeating, particularly as it has parallels with a number of clubs including Southampton, Lyon and Feyenoord. The German federation's clear and coherent long-term plan was eventually translated into World Cup victory in 2014; with the fact that it relied on youth only increasing its sustainability.

We often feel that there's a strong connection between experience and success, and so consequently favour older players at critical moments. But with the bravery to execute their succession plan, Germany showed that youth and experience needn't be mutually exclusive.

Now they have the medals to show for it.

When Time Catches Up with Our Players

In order to build success, it is key to understand the age at which players perform at their peak. Unfortunately, it is also a neglected area of research, partly owing to difficulties in measuring player development.

While there are numerous performance indicators that we can monitor, playing time may still be the best alternative; a player who is rarely selected can perhaps be considered a less valuable asset. Blind spots do exist, although invariably players are not in contention owing to a relative lack of talent or age-related decline.

By looking at teams which played at least four seasons in the Premier League between 1998 and 2014, we can see if a side's age profile (how minutes were spread across different ages) is correlated to achievement.

For example, Arsenal's best performance in those years was their undefeated 2003/04 season, while their worst came in 2005/06, when they finished fourth. We can compare the age profiles between their best and worst seasons, and repeat this process for all other teams.

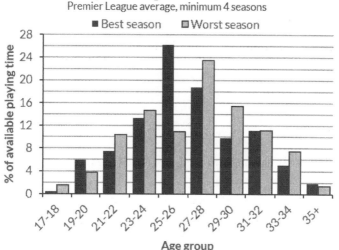

Striker playing time by age group for best and worst-performing team seasons
Premier League average, minimum 4 seasons

Different playing positions have different peak ages, but the trend is clear for strikers. When averaged across all teams, 25 and 26 year olds accounted for almost a quarter of the playing time for strikers from teams enjoying their best seasons.

Defenders and midfielders in football see similar differences between teams enjoying their best and worst campaigns. In unsuccessful seasons, defenders aged over 30 were far more prominent, whilst in successful seasons midfields were dominated by 25 to 26 year olds.

Too often we select, renew and buy players on past success rather than likely future productivity. This is often done for sentimental reasons, or a mistaken belief that the past accurately predicts the future. As evidence of this, 28 and 29-year-old players accounted for over 26% of the playing time given to strikers by sides that were enduring their least successful season.

Of course, circumstances vary by club. Limited squad sizes, short term goals and financial constraints mean it is sometimes necessary to select players who retain some of their past ability, despite being beyond their peak. Experience also brings other qualities, particularly in terms of leadership. However, clubs must endeavour to look within, promoting young prospects who can mature into their peak years and represent a more cost effective option in succession planning.

Clubs often ask us what the age profile of a winning team is. By assessing the lifecycle of teams during their best and worst seasons, we can identify peak talent for each position. We can therefore be better informed about exactly how loading a team with age-declining talent – either through necessity or design – can impact a club's ability to win.

III: PERFORMANCE

Football, Not Moneyball

The so-called 'Moneyball' approach has been the recipient of a significant amount of media criticism in recent times. Whether it be Liverpool's much-publicised transfer committee or Brentford's supposed total reliance on data, the Moneyball tag has come to have strong negative connotations in football.

But let's take a moment. Moneyball was the name of a book written by Michael Lewis (later turned into a Hollywood movie starring Brad Pitt) about a relatively poor baseball team that was able to punch above its weight by thinking differently in terms of player trading.

Somewhere along the way, however, the story of Moneyball has been twisted, distorted and generalised to become a catch-all phrase for the use of data in football. Moneyball has become misrepresented and is in need of a serious brand overhaul.

Here's the thing: football is an unpredictable and nuanced sport. Because of its low-scoring nature, the better team on the day often fails to win (about 40% of the time, according to our analysis). Football is an unfair game, which of course is what makes it thrillingly – and often exasperatingly – brilliant.

Data won't change this (nor should we want it to), but it can be used to gain a deeper understanding of the 'why' and nudge the odds in your favour. Used to its full potential, data can help to create constructive accountability around your club's own long-term purpose. It allows us to look probabilistically at your talent pool and create effective succession pathways for the next generation. It can make us smarter in the transfer market. It's not all about counting shots, passes, crosses nor the distance covered.

This is football, not Moneyball.

I Cannot Make Bricks Without Clay!

"Data, data, data!" [Holmes] cried impatiently. "I cannot make bricks without clay!"
(Sir Arthur Conan Doyle, The Adventure of the Copper Beeches)

The brilliant detective of Conan Doyle's creation is not alone. Today, key decision-makers in most fields rely on a healthy supply of data to make the decisions on which their organisation depends. They see the value of using objective information to challenge their thinking or validate their intuition. They seek to understand its limitations to ensure that it can be deployed most effectively.

Take driving as an example. Few would claim that road-use data has improved people's inherent ability to safely manoeuvre a car, but:

- It has helped insurers price their products more accurately

- It has helped car manufacturers improve the safety of their designs

- It has changed the way roads are set up to ensure danger spots are minimised

- It has helped governments establish the best approach to applying speed limits and traffic regulation

- It has helped positively influence the design of a public transport system

In football, critics often point to the limitations of analytics without an appreciation of the extent to which data evaluation can help. It may be true that analytics can't effectively measure defensive output (yet), nor can it make your players more talented, but:

- It can encourage specific training approaches

- It can help you assess which tactics might work best

- It can improve your strike rate in the transfer market

- It can stop you unnecessarily sacking your manager

- It can help you select the best manager for your club

- It can assist with effective future planning

It is clearly important to appreciate the limitations of analytics – data poorly applied often does more harm than good – but sometimes you have to tolerate imperfection to drive for a better outcome.

Who Else is Doing This?

Football is enjoying an age of unprecedented innovation. New thinking and new technologies run through the sport, though many areas for development remain untapped.

When confronted with a new software, idea or opportunity, clubs will often ask, "Who else is doing this?"

A club might ask this for one of two reasons:

Some clubs want case studies and fall victim to social proofing. They want to keep pace with their rivals and are fearful of being left behind.

Others want to hear that nobody else is doing this and be assured that they're the first mover. They want a competitive edge on their rivals and seek to have the upper hand.

Knowing what other clubs are doing is useful. Knowing what other clubs aren't doing is advantageous.

Why Intuition Needn't be a Dirty Word

In September 2014, Mike Goodman wrote an excellent summary of the state of football analytics. Providing a snapshot of advances in the area, Goodman made the crucial distinction between data and analytics; the former telling what happened, and the latter helping to explain what is likely happen.

There was one paragraph of Goodman's article, on Total Shots Ratio (the ratio of how many shots a team takes versus the number of total shots), that stuck out. Goodman wrote:

"Total Shots Ratio (TSR) is incredibly helpful when it comes to figuring out what teams might do well in any given season (though, of course, some dumb writers will ignore it and pick Manchester United to finish third), but it isn't all that helpful when it comes to actually managing a team."

What Goodman means is that TSR is a team metric; it doesn't tell a manager which players are duds and which are winners, or what kind of tactics the team should be employing.

But I disagree that basic predictive metrics like TSR aren't "all that helpful to actually managing a team."

Here's a simple example:

A Premier League team is climbing the table with three wins and a draw to start the season but posting a TSR of .458. This information isn't very helpful in isolation, but can be compared to the team's PDO, a number representing shot percentage plus save percentage. Because this metric tends to regress to the mean very quickly, a high or low PDO can reveal the influence of luck. This particular team has a league-high PDO of 1489. We can break that number down into a shot percentage of 60% and a save percentage of 88.9%. These are extremely unsustainable numbers, particularly the shooting percentage. So, with a low TSR and a high PDO, the simple conclusion is that the team is riding their luck.

If you're a betting person, you can make quick use of this information, but if you're a performance analyst at a club, what do you do with it? On the one hand, you might concede that the information is incomplete, but it's still something. If I know that a low TSR is generally going to mean a lower points total as the season progresses, I might look for clues as why my team is, as a rule, conceding more shots than they're taking.

Finding those clues is a process that involves both analytics and intuition based on tactical understanding, experience, and reviews of past performances. 'Intuition' needn't be a dirty word. The problem with both supporters and detractors of sports analytics is they expect predictive metrics to do all or nothing. For example, if TSR can't tell you which formation to use or which starting XI to select, it is branded useless.

However, simply knowing there is a fundamental problem with a club despite positive results can be the difference between a manager telling a team to "keep up the good work," and a manager carefully working with players and staff to find constructive, tactically-grounded ways to help improve overall performance.

Football analytics, even at this early stage in its development, can still be a vital tool as clubs seek to improve season-on-season. We shouldn't put more expectation on analytics than they can bear, but clubs should embrace new ways of achieving competitive edge.

Why You're Not Only as Good as Your Last Game

"You have to put it into perspective…we just came out of two convincing results at Bayern Munich and Tottenham with a very solid defensive performance, so you have to think that was an accident…that doesn't mean that you're not a good driver. It just means we have played about 40 games this season and it's not what happened on Saturday that reflects the quality of this team."
(Arsène Wenger, March 2014)

Arsenal fans may not have agreed with their club's manager after he made those comments following Chelsea's 6-0 defeat of The Gunners in March 2014, but the Frenchman was right.

What Wenger was referring to is essentially the performance versus results debate. It's easy to mistake one for the other, but they are in fact very different; performance represents the actions you take and how you execute them, whereas the result is what you get at the end of the performance (plus other factors, such as luck, which is particularly relevant in a footballing context).

Few, including Wenger, would suggest that Arsenal played well or deserved a result from the Chelsea game, but context is key in these situations. Sports teams and businesses should always assess long-term underlying performance, as opposed to short-term (and often superficial) results. In this way, and staying with Wenger's car crash metaphor, results can sometimes be explained as merely a bump in the road for a team heading in the right direction.

The Thing About That Win

...is that you may not have deserved it.

Alternatively, you may have lost a game that you didn't deserve to lose.

Consider this analogy: two students are preparing for an exam, which has three questions. One studies the entire syllabus, all six topics, safe in the knowledge that she has all bases covered. The other, less able student studies three topics in the hope that the questions will fall his way. On the day of the exam, the three topics the second student revised for appear in the paper and both students score high marks. The outcome is the same, but only one of the students truly deserved it. The other was lucky, and on another day the outcome would have been different.

When a result goes your way, it's tempting to believe that your performance warranted the victory. Conversely, it's all too easy to justify reactionary changes after a defeat. "You're only as good as your last game", as the saying goes.

But here's the thing: football is a low scoring sport, which invariably means that luck plays its part and teams don't necessarily get what they deserve in the short-term. In nearly half of all games, the result doesn't go the way the balance of play would suggest it should.

What if we told you that a Premier League team secured 13 more points than their performances deserved during the first half of the 2014/15 season? Or that a team in the Bundesliga were 12 places below where they should have been mid-way through the campaign?

Sometimes the league table *does* lie.

When we only focus on results, we can miscalculate the need for change and make rash decisions. Instead, focusing on performance helps us to achieve a true gauge of the underlying, sustainable strength of our team.

In the long-run, our statistical model suggests that performance (measured by focusing on process over outcome) is a better predictor of league table position than results. In the short-term, performance and luck can combine to achieve good results. However, in the long-term performance alone will determine a team's fortunes.

When is a Crisis Not a Crisis?

When things aren't going your way, it can be difficult to stay calm and take an objective view of events. It can be equally hard to look beyond the league table and realise that results don't tell the full story.

We often hear managers defend poor results in their post-match interviews. "We played well, but it just didn't go for us today," they might say. This can seem like an excuse, leaving owners and fans exasperated. Ultimately, however, they know that it is results and not performances that put points on the board. As anxiety kicks in, panic and hysteria can escalate quickly. When the results still don't come, even the most self-assured managers will start to question themselves, even if they feel that performances are of a satisfactory level. The sensation is similar to struggling in a pool game against a complete novice; you know you're the stronger player at the table, but none of your shots are dropping as everything goes in for your lucky opponent.

As an example, let's revisit Newcastle United's situation during the early part of the 2014/15 Premier League season.

After six games, Newcastle were 19th in the table with just three points and having scored only five goals, conceding 12. On the face of it, the club were experiencing relegation form. However, we can take a deeper look at the club's performances during that time using a unique model that assesses a team's effectiveness at critical attacking and defensive moments during matches.

Our analysis reveals that Newcastle's early season performances were not as bad as results suggested. They may have only scored five goals, but our model shows that they were getting into the right positions and had probably been unfortunate not to score more. We know this because past data tells us that a typical team in the same shooting positions would have scored with 9% of their attempts, while Newcastle managed just 5% (equivalent to 2.8 goals less than we'd expect from their chances created).

While critics will argue that they should have been more clinical, there is always a context; a near miss, a shot against the post, or a miraculous save from the opposition goalkeeper. History shows that teams do not remain this wasteful or unlucky in the long run. The important thing for Newcastle was that they were creating chances and, with a bit more luck in front of goal, may well have converted at least one of their three draws into a victory.

At the other end of the pitch, Newcastle had conceded 12 goals at an average of two per match, the third worst record in the league. However, their opponents had been extremely clinical, converting 18% of their shots (almost double the Premier League average of 10%). Such offensive efficiency from opponents was always unlikely to continue across the entirety of the season, as was illustrated by Newcastle eventually finishing in 15th place.

Although Newcastle sat 19th in the league after six games, they actually ranked 8th in terms of performance. In fact, in 95% of the simulations we ran, Newcastle would have secured equal or better overall results from the same performances.

The Newcastle example aside, every team can benefit from looking at the bigger picture. When faced with a perceived crisis, clubs must try to see past the hysteria and take a long-term view. Of course, if the underlying performances on the pitch are poor, then it could be time for a change. However, if your performances are OK, then history tells us that the results will come.

Four Defending Champions

A title defence is quite rightly regarded as one of football's toughest feats. Across European football during the 2015/16 season, we saw different teams approach the challenge with varying levels of success.

It can be easy to get swept up in simplistic narratives that exaggerate or conceal the need for change. 'Winning ugly', 'suffering from complacency' and 'lacking motivation' are all stock phrases associated with defending champions that obscure a more complex reality.

The top leagues in Germany, Denmark, Italy and England all saw title defences of varying quality in 2015/16. As some narratives held true, others were skewed by football's propensity for outliers. In many cases, results are better explained through quantifiable measures. Tools such as 21st Club's Performance League can be used to more accurately estimate the strength of each team.

In Germany and England, Bayern Munich's and Chelsea's seasons took opposing courses thanks to clearly contrasting performance levels. In Denmark and Italy, however, the previous season's champions suffered from discrepancies between performances and results.

By mid-November, Juventus' underlying defensive numbers – fewer than nine shots conceded per game, mostly from unfavourable positions – saw 21st Club calculate that they still had a 16% chance of overhauling a nine-point deficit to become champions once again. Juve duly went on a magnificent run of form and won the league by nine points from Napoli.

FC Midtjylland, meanwhile, were just a point off the pace in Denmark in November despite their rivals' ascendancy in underlying metrics. As expected, Midtjylland dropped off and eventually finished third, 12 points behind champions Copenhagen.

False Dominance FC Midtjylland Denmark Actual 2nd Performance 3rd Finished 3rd	**Deserved Leaders** Bayern München Germany Actual 1st Performance 1st Finished 1st
Troubled Times Chelsea England Actual 16th Performance 13th Finished 10th	**False Decline** Juventus Italy Actual 7th Performance 1st Finished 1st

Actual and performance positions reflect values on 13th November 2015

These explanations needn't just apply to teams competing at the sharp end of the league, they apply to all teams attempting to reach or exceed benchmarks set during the previous season. Using predictive metrics alongside the league table can help to clarify true performance levels and contextualise the outlook for the rest of the season.

When a Champion Looks Like a Loser

The conventional wisdom at the end of a season is that 'the league table never lies'; that the best team will be champions and the worst team will finish bottom.

This wisdom, however, is a contradiction to the comments we routinely hear after tight matches. "I thought we were the better team" or "I thought we got a bit lucky" have become stock answers to post-match questions. In 2014/15, one missed penalty from Derby County pushed them out of the play-off places, but didn't instantly turn them into only the division's eighth-best team. During the same season, Bundesliga strugglers Freiburg beat Bayern Munich; a result that didn't suddenly mean the team were good enough to stay up.

It's also perfectly possible for the best team in the league to have things not go their way over an entire season and fail to finish as champions. There's no law that ensures fortune evens itself out over a ten-month period; in a low-scoring sport, there's no reason why a good team can't lose for weeks on end. Our analysis shows that a Premier League team that has all the underlying traits of previous league winners would expect to win the title around 60% of the time. In one in every four seasons the title would go to the side that is actually the second-best team in the division.

At the bottom, it's not impossible for the worst team in the league to stay up, simply by things going their way. In the Premier League, we'd expect this to happen 20% of the time, whilst a team good enough to finish 13th on average has as good a chance of finishing bottom as it does fifth.

In the English Championship, a far more competitive division, the best team can expect to win the league just 50% of the time, with the worst team relegated only 70% of the time.

When dealing with such noisy information it's vital to have a true measure of how good our team really is. The table might suggest we're a top-four contender, but the reality is our underlying performance is that of a mid-table side. Equally, it's important not to panic when results don't go our way.

Contrary to received wisdom, the league table almost *always* lies.

The Barcelona Problem

April 2016 was a difficult month for Barcelona. Three consecutive league defeats and a Champions League exit saw the Catalan giants installed as the crisis club of the moment. Such extreme outlying results – the odds of Barcelona enduring such a miserable run were around 2,500 to 1 – at any club demand serious examination.

The first step for clubs in this situation is to get an objective, baseline view of performance from which to begin the analysis. By doing this for Barcelona, we can see that their league performances in April 2016 would typically have returned 5.8 points based on the quality and quantity of chances created and allowed. This is slightly worse than the 6.8 points expected before the run, but by no means catastrophic. Meanwhile, their Champions League quarter-final first leg performance against Atlético Madrid would typically have returned at least a two-goal win around 50% of the time, rather than the slender one-goal lead Luis Enrique's team actually took to the second leg.

Barcelona's 'crisis' can broadly be put down to a run of poor finishing. A reasonable interpretation of the statistics suggests that such runs are a part of football's natural variation and usually end sooner rather than later. But there may be more to it than that.

The Times' Gabriele Marcotti noted how Lionel Messi, Luis Suárez and Neymar had all played over 250 hours of football from April 2015 to April 2016, something that could have contributed to tiredness and poor execution in attacking areas. Others mentioned how defences had dropped deeper against Barcelona, or referenced the toll Johan Cruyff's death took on the squad.

The point is that all these theories provide a starting point for further analysis; they can help us better comprehend the real reasons why things are happening, or if there is even a problem at all. From that, we can make decisions that are based on evidence rather than assumption, strategy rather than reactivity. The problems experienced by Barcelona in April 2016 are, at some point, every club's problems. Fortunately, there's a simple diagnostic that can help deliver answers.

What Would You do if You Were Dortmund?

Football creates outliers like no other sport. A miscued shot here, a marginal refereeing decision there, and before long it's no wins in 'x' games, or no goals in 'y' hours.

Most outliers find their way back to earth, their tether being reeled in by the forces of probability. But for Borussia Dortmund in 2014/15, the tether took six months to go taut; results spinning out of control until the team finally began to turn things around in February.

And yet, despite a horrendous few months, the manager's position was never questioned, the players remained loyal, and the fans kept coming through the turnstiles. The club remained united in the face of adversity.

Using 21st Club's Performance League model to look under the bonnet, it was possible to see that Dortmund's underlying performance was still of a top-four standard, that despite suffering 11 defeats in their first 19 league games. They were creating good chances and didn't afford many to their opponents. Their goal difference was 14 goals worse than it should have been in early February. Results looked set to improve and duly did.

To an outsider, Dortmund appears to be a club built on trust. To represent, support, or play for Dortmund is not a transient experience. There is no short-termism or panic.

Would we react the same way at our own clubs? Would we confuse urgency with panic?

What would you have done if you were Dortmund?

Copying Spain

Between 2008 and 2012, Barcelona and Spain's possession-heavy playing style led to unparalleled domestic and international success. As a result, the European game experienced a significant tactical shift that was driven by a desire to mimic the best aspects of those teams.

People also noticed that Spain and Barcelona were winning trophies with players well under six feet (183 cm) tall. Consciously or otherwise, other national teams followed suit. In fact, our analysis shows that the average height of international footballers has fallen by a couple of centimetres in recent years.

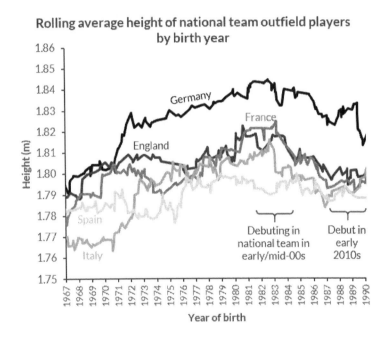

These tactical and physical trends illustrate how football often finds it much easier to follow the crowd and copy what seems to be working elsewhere. Too often this is done at the cost of disregarding what is suitable for one's own situation. This doesn't just apply to tactics or youth development; over the years we've seen teams playing catch up in approaches in areas such as sports science, recruitment and analytics.

Developing a clear philosophy has obvious benefits, even if it means going against the grain. If we're not developing our own way of doing things, we can be sure that as long as we're following the trend, our competitors are opening up new avenues for success.

Where do We Rank?

In February 2015, ESPN released a feature entitled 'The Great Analytics Rankings'. In it they rated every major US sports franchise on its "analytics staff, its buy-in from execs and coaches, its investment in biometric data, and how much its approach is predicated on analytics," producing a top 10, bottom 10, and a headline assessment of each team.

It would be difficult to perform a similarly comprehensive overview of the competition at a professional sports club, but there is enough knowledge exchanged within the industry to at least hazard a guess.

Grab a flipchart and pen and title the page with a specific area of operations. It might be Analytics, but it could easily be Recruitment, Youth Development, Succession Planning or Fan Engagement. Then start to make a list, maybe of clubs in your league, country, or of teams you consider to be direct competition.

From top to bottom, rank the teams from best to worst in the area in question. Identify where your team ranks, and how far ahead a theoretical "perfect club" would be.

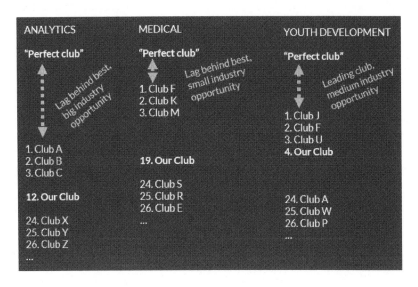

In our fictitious example, we are furthest behind the top-ranked teams in the area of medical, but the biggest industry opportunity is in analytics, given that the best club is far from having the theoretical perfect operation in this area. In youth development, despite being one of the industry leaders, there's still plenty of headroom for even the best teams to improve.

Given finite resources, the choice then becomes:

1. Should we attempt to catch up with our competitors by improving in areas where we are weak? Or,

2. Should we attempt to gain a competitive advantage by improving in areas where our competitors are weak?

There is no correct answer; different areas will have different and unpredictable levels of impact on first-team performance. At the very least, however, this exercise can help us understand if we're neglecting areas where the marginal gains could be massive, or overspending in areas where each extra dollar has a negligible effect.

Pin your rankings to the office wall and see where you lie in six months' time.

The Unknown Truth

The story of the 2015/16 season in European football was the rise of Leicester City. After winning 41 points in 2014/15, they won 81 points in 2015/16 as they secured the unlikeliest of league titles.

Leicester were a clear case of a team being knowingly better, vastly improving on 2014/15 both in terms of results and underlying performance. Chelsea were the Foxes' mirror image; a team that won the title in 2014/15 only to become knowingly worse the following year as they finished in tenth place.

But across Europe there were some teams that were unknowingly better or worse. These are teams who appear to have improved or regressed, but have performance levels that suggest results should have gone in a different direction. If all else remains relatively constant for teams in those situations, results will likely trend towards the expected performance level.

These teams are often the most vulnerable to decisions that go against the club's apparent needs (or lack thereof). In 2015/16, Montpellier and Rayo Vallecano, for example, may have been tempted into wholesale changes after surprise flirtations with relegation (Rayo did end up being relegated), when in reality underlying performance had improved from 2014/15. Things simply didn't go their way.

On the flip side, seemingly successful 2015/16 seasons for Inter, Mainz and Villarreal were built on foundations that are actually shakier than the previous campaigns. In Inter's case, their good early form began to subside in January and February as the club slipped from first to fifth, eventually finishing fourth. In the long run, you are more likely to get what you deserve.

Sometimes these counter-intuitive outcomes can seem impossible; there will always be some clubs somewhere that in isolation appear to be outliers. Knowing what to do in these unusual circumstances can help prevent fatal over- or under-reactions.

The Underdog Theory

The first week of May 2016 was a remarkable time for footballing underdogs. On Monday 2nd May, Leicester City completed their astonishing title charge, while Atlético Madrid reached a second Champions League final in three years just 24 hours later.

Theories abound as to the reasons for their success, ranging from team spirit to the degree of luck each enjoyed. A discussion of these is too long for this particular article, but one notable aspect is the distinctiveness of each club's playing style relative to their closest rivals.

The theory goes that, to beat the best, you have to do something different. This is especially true for clubs with limited resources. On the field, neither Leicester nor Atléti resemble the slick, sophisticated styles of Europe's richest clubs. Their modus operandi are to disrupt their opponents, in much the same way successful start-ups shake up entire industries; think Uber or Airbnb. Leicester and Atlético play guerilla football.

Off the field, much has been written about management style and the search for competitive edge. Understanding this, coupled with a study of the teams that have tried to be different but failed, will only help broaden the lessons to be learnt from the unprecedented achievements of 2015/16.

While the football world follows the most fashionable trends, Leicester City and Atlético Madrid dared to be different. That in itself is deserving of appreciation.

Taking Stock

During the season, we spend so much time in 'push mode' that we can forget to celebrate what went well, or to evaluate why. We typically tend to take stock only at the end of the season, when we finally get a chance to come up for air.

Ideally, pre-season expectations will have been set against goals which enable an objective review process. However, in the absence of pre-defined targets, an effective method of assessing the season is to review a club's performance relative to resources.

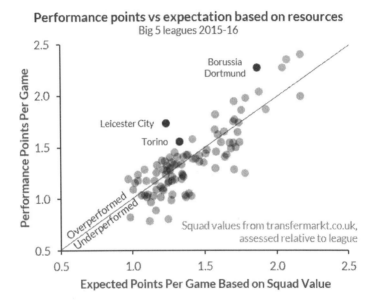

Perhaps unsurprisingly, this alternative perspective validates the achievements of both Leicester City and Borussia Dortmund during the 2015/16 season. Interestingly, this approach can also highlight the performances of teams that may have slipped under the radar; Torino, for example. Despite finishing 12th in Serie A, Torino demonstrated impressive underlying performance levels that notably exceeded the expectations we might set by the value of their squad.

Whether it's early in the season or approaching the conclusion, there is never a bad time to structure a performance review that goes deeper than the often misleading league standings. In a highly competitive environment, success next season may hinge on developing a true understanding of what happened – and why – this year.

The Second Season Illusion

In June 2010, Birmingham City manager Alex McLeish vowed that his club – which had just finished an impressive ninth in the Premier League following promotion – would not fall victim to 'second season syndrome'.

"We will do some homework regarding teams that struggled a bit in their second years to see if we can pinpoint one or two things to help us from their experiences," said McLeish. "We will leave no stone unturned and also get the right psychological messages to the players."

Unfortunately for Birmingham – and countless other teams over the years – the odds were stacked against them, but for the reasons often given in the media. The narrative that goes with second season syndrome is that it's the result of teams being 'worked out' by opponents, or players losing motivation. The reality is that this apparent affliction is chiefly explained by a statistical phenomenon known as regression to the mean.

Despite finishing ninth, only one team conceded more shots inside the area than Birmingham City during the 2009/10 Premier League season. They were by no means world-beaters in front of goal, either. Their success, therefore, was built upon alarming opponent wastefulness: just 7.1% of opponent shots were scored, compared to a league average of 9.7%. For all of on-loan Joe Hart's heroics in goal, these were not the numbers of a mid-table team. Ultimately, Birmingham's performance levels were not sustainable.

The following season, Birmingham did indeed suffer second season syndrome, finishing 18th with 11 fewer points and 11 more goals against. They conceded virtually the same number of shots inside the area as the previous season, but their opponents merely started scoring their chances at the average rate.

That is not to say that psychological factors do not play a part in this phenomenon; it is just that they are far less important and predictable than traditional wisdom accepts. Teams and players that have avoided second season syndrome were typically those that had strong underlying numbers and were not riding a bubble of success.

So if your striker is in a slump, or your team just can't seem to build on the surprise results of last year, remember that second season syndrome can be predicted, and you can identify the true causes before the problem strikes.

The Motivation Equation

When a transfer window closes, attention turns to maximising the potential of the existing playing squad.

One of the ways clubs can do this is by implementing a bonus structure, with players rewarded for appearances, wins, or performance in various competitions. These bonuses are incentives designed to encourage players to perform at an even higher level than they normally would.

Bonuses are combined with the primary incentive to perform – the stakes of competition – to create the motivation equation for a footballer:

$$\text{Motivation} = \text{League Situation Incentive} + \text{Monetary Incentive}$$

However, consider a situation where, in a limp end-of-season performance, commentators and managers bemoan that players "had nothing to play for" or "no motivation to win the game".

If players "have no motivation" in any given match, it stands to reason that both the league situation and the monetary incentive had no effect on a player's urgency to perform. If monetary incentives have no effect in meaningless end-of-season games – when they should be the only thing on a player's mind – are we still to believe they have an effect at the start or in the middle of the season?

Of course, bonuses are also used to attract players and mitigate risk, but their primary purpose should surely be to change behaviour and positively influence performance during the season.

Whilst team-level bonuses must be agreed before the season, there is always the opportunity to reconsider player contract structures and ask ourselves whether the bonuses we're paying our players are really helping us win.

Burnout: Perception and Planning

In October 2014, Raheem Sterling's request not to start England's Euro 2016 qualifying game against Estonia because of tiredness brought the topic of burnout to the fore.

There were two sides to the debate that raged in the media: those giving credit to Sterling for being mature enough to speak up and give Roy Hodgson the choice, and those left baffled by a 19-year-old being too tired to want to play for England at a relatively early stage of the season.

Whichever side of the argument you might have been on, it is evident that injuries are an unfortunate side-effect of having international-class players in your squad, and that clubs are often left counting the cost of the international break.

The issue of overuse, however, is slightly different. The notion is that too much football will lead to residual fatigue snowballing into increased risk of injury – hence why we need to protect our most talented young players. It is a case of prevention rather than cure.

This makes intuitive sense from a sports science perspective, except that there doesn't seem to be much evidence to show that young Premier League players do burnout if used too much. 21st Club's research has analysed season-to-season usage rates for players under the age of 21 to look for signs of burnout.

If young players were prone to burnout, we would expect to see a greater percentage of them moving from being a core player (more than 50% of minutes played) one season, to being a squad or fringe player (less than 50% of minutes played) the next – just like Seamus Coleman did at Everton from 2010/11 to 2011/12. However, this isn't the case. In fact, 35% of core players aged under 22 were 'relegated' to squad or fringe status the following season, either through injury or a lack of selection. This sounds like a lot, but in fact it is exactly the same rate as those aged 22 or older.

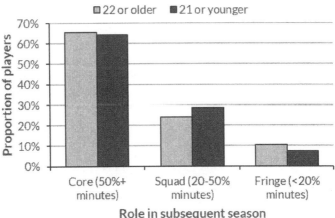

Role of retained 'core' players in subsequent season
Premier League 2008-2013

There's always a context, but the data infers that there's a lot of squad churn irrespective of age profile. This is likely to be as much about being displaced by new signings than burning out. It's dog eat dog, and only the strongest will survive.

Assuming they stay injury free, the best players will play more minutes with each passing season. This is simply because they are good enough and ultimately clubs are keen to see their best young talent come through the system. In Sterling's case, over the three seasons from 2012/13 to 2014/15, he played 51%, 65% and 89% of minutes respectively.

While protection is a sensible approach, it's equally important to create clear pathways to enable player development. In order to achieve that, we need a framework to forecast how much reliance there will be on young core players like Sterling. This is just one of the many reasons why 21st Club works with teams to plan for the future and maximise their potential

IV: PLANNING

Football's Ticking Clock

"Time management is an oxymoron. Time is beyond our control, and the clock keeps ticking regardless of how we lead our lives. Priority management is the answer to maximising the time we have."
(John C. Maxwell)

During the hectic football season, priority management is the order of the day.

Consider the analogy of the ticking clock.

Imagine that each of the clock's hands represents a task you need to fulfill during the season.

Think of the characteristics of the second hand; continuously moving, always happening, forever ticking. Picture that the second hand represents the next league game coming around fast, waiting for no one.

Now consider the minute hand. It moves slower than the second hand, although it's still creeping around the clock face and taking our time. In a football context, imagine that the minute hand represents the transfer window, or perhaps a less incessant competition like the FA Cup.

Finally, picture the hour hand. Imagine this hand represents long-term development, future horizon scanning and squad succession planning. The hour hand moves much slower than the minute and second hands, but when it does move it makes the biggest impact.

The important point is that all three of the clock's hands move simultaneously. There can be no avoiding the next match or the short-term need to secure results. If the second hand stopped moving, then the minute and hour hands wouldn't function at all. But equally we must make time for the long-term processes that help us plan for the future and build sustainable success.

So our challenge becomes about how we prioritise tasks – either individually or collectively – within our club.

It is true that time waits for no one, but we are in control of how we use it.

Urgent vs Important

"What is important is seldom urgent and what is urgent is seldom important."
(Dwight D. Eisenhower)

Your next match is urgent.

Your position at the end of the season is important.

Dealing with a disappointing result from the weekend is urgent, understanding if you actually deserved to lose is important.

Signing a new player in the window is urgent, creating pathways for the next generation is important.

The age profile of your squad today is urgent, developing a succession plan that ensures a continuous availability of peak age players is important.

Adopting a playing strategy for the weekend is urgent, building a philosophy for the club is important.

Getting our heads down and working hard is urgent, getting an outside view is important.

The characteristics of important are strategic, long-term, enduring, foundational, stable and meaningful.

If we invest in important, urgent happens less often. The inverse is seldom true.

The Scarcity Trap

Oliver Burkeman is Busy, the eponymous journalist's 2016 BBC Radio Four miniseries on the subject of busyness, provided a number of insights into how difficult it can be to manage our time amidst the distractions of modern life.

In one of the episodes, Eldar Shafir, Professor of Psychology at the University of Princeton, talks about a phenomenon known as 'the scarcity trap':

"When you're busy and have limited bandwidth, you start making decisions less well. It's called the scarcity trap. As you are overwhelmed with doing more and more, you have less time to think carefully about how to do each task."

In football, as we are constantly distracted by a weekly cycle of matches and short-term decisions, it can be difficult to find the time for contemplation and big-picture strategic thinking.

Shafir has a remedy for this common problem called "meeting with self", a solution that encourages people to set aside two 15 or 30 minute chunks of time each day. This time is to be used to take care of unexpected tasks or to ruminate over long-term strategic issues. Not only does this enable a healthier approach to time management, it also affords us the flexibility and space required for clear thinking free from distraction.

A similar approach can be applied at an organisational level. It can be tempting to focus solely on short-term results, but ultimately overarching strategic decisions will have a greater bearing on the future health of a club. Make sure that the key decision-makers in your club are regularly finding the time to step back from their daily tasks and think reflectively about the direction of the organisation.

If you can avoid the scarcity trap, you'll be in a far better position to make effective decisions that influence both the present and future of your club.

Three Ways to Approach the Future

Here are three ways for football clubs to approach and plan for the future:

1. Predict

If you can make accurate forecasts about the future, then prediction is the most rewarding approach. It enables you to gain an advantage by being the first to move as a result of your understanding of tomorrow.

The influence of luck makes football difficult to predict, although it is possible to forecast the likely future performance of a team by adopting a probabilistic approach. Individual talent is arguably trickier to predict, but there are ways to estimate which young players might break through the pack, enabling you to capitalise on your talent pool.

2. Evolve

If you can admit that it's not possible to predict the future with certainty, then evolution is a good approach. Evolution is about planning, testing, re-evaluating and experiencing breakthroughs. This may seem indulgent in the winner-takes-all culture of elite football, but it has long-term benefits.

The key is not to make your approach too broad; if you allow for every possible future scenario then you may lose out to a teams that focus on a smaller number of areas. Hence, focused evolution is best for building an effective framework for squad development.

3. Avoid

Assuming that tomorrow's world will be like today's is a third approach, but not a particularly clever one. However, in football it is an approach we see far too frequently.

Avoidance is letting the second hand of the ticking clock dictate your life; it's short-sighted and will block the talent pathway for the next generation of players.

As you plan for the future, the best way to prepare is by finding the right blend of prediction and evolution.

Four Facts

Four facts you should consider when planning for the future:

1. The league table often lies

Because football is such a low scoring sport, teams don't always get the results they deserve. In December 2015, for example, Werder Bremen sat 16th in the Bundesliga despite being the 11th best performing team according to our statistical model. It was therefore unsurprising when they climbed up the table during the second half of the season, eventually finishing 13th. Without a true marker of underlying performance, clubs tend to over- or underestimate the need for change.

2. You're at your best when your players hit peak age

Research into Premier League age profiles reveals that clubs often have their best seasons when the bulk of their squad is made up of peak age players (25-28, depending on position), and their worst seasons when they have too many old and/or young players. It's not always easy to keep hold of your best players during their peak years, but doing so would improve your chances of success.

3. It pays to invest in younger players

On average, 24-year-olds are already at 98% of their peak value, meaning their future value is likely to increase only slightly (peaking at around 25) before declining. By 30, a player will have depreciated to 76% of his once peak market value. By 32, it's 54%. By all means invest in experience, but know that a player's value will steadily decline after their 25th birthday.

4. We continue to confuse age with talent

In the big five European leagues in 2015/16, 31% of players were born in the first quarter of the year and just 17% in the last quarter. This means that we're potentially missing out on a huge crop of late-born youngsters, overlooked by talent spotters who see older as better.

It's not easy to predict the future, but it is possible to nudge the odds in your favour.

Succession Planning and Future-Proofing

In the future, it will be the norm for elite clubs to have informed, comprehensive succession plans in place. These plans will incorporate everything from projected player market values to on-field metrics to keep track of areas of strength and weakness in the squad. Regular horizon scanning will also help improve the transition of academy players into the first team, as the succession plan identifies key areas for youth coaches to work on and shore up any weaknesses in the first team.

Most importantly, these plans will ensure that everyone at the club has a collective idea of the organisation's long and short term strategy to deal with even the most unexpected and unlikely outcomes. These plans will also help prevent the kind of knee-jerk, reactionary transfer decisions that can put clubs at unnecessary competitive and financial risk.

Today, however, many clubs simply don't have a succession planning strategy in place. Witness the response to the April 2014 news that FIFA had handed Barcelona a two window transfer ban for alleged violations of transfer regulations. There was not only confusion in the press over the status of deals for Alen Halilovic and Marc-Andre ter Stegen, but concern over potential replacements for the ageing Carles Puyol in defense.

Yet Barcelona was first alerted to the investigation in February 2013, 14 months ahead of FIFA's disciplinary ruling. This should have given the club ample time to make contingency plans for replacing key members of the squad, with consideration given to the worst case scenario of a transfer ban.

Whereas Barcelona's case may be an outlier, there are other areas where a strong succession plan would have made a significant difference. Some analysts point to weaknesses in Manchester United's first team stretching back to before their 2012/13 title-winning season, and argue that David Moyes walked into the United job with very little time to make crucial changes. It's not clear whether United knew of these potential issues, yet Moyes' comment that he was still short of quality first team players less than a month after the end of the 2013 summer transfer window points to the absence of an adequate succession plan for an ageing squad.

Some argue that these decisions should be left to the manager alone, but as we've seen with United, this can lead to instability and 'transitional' seasons, leading to a loss of revenue. A strong succession plan ensures decisions that influence the fate of expensive squad assets, rather than being made by one person, are a collaborative process involving all key stakeholders. These plans also help avoid the loss of an entire season due to a handful of failed deals for players in key positions, something which even the most skilled directors and managers can't always prevent.

Ensuring these succession plans are regularly updated and adapted to changing circumstances will be made easier with cutting edge software, too. However, for clubs with modest resources, simply making time for regular meetings between key decision makers to discuss the future direction of the team will make a big difference in shifting organisational planning from the short to the long term. It can also be crucial in helping to prevent the kind of panic-driven mistakes that clubs sometimes pay for years down the line.

The Essence of Succession Planning

Each year, FIFPro – the representative body for professional footballers – reveals its World XI as voted for by its 20,000 members. The team is a selection of the greatest talent the game has to offer and gets fans dreaming about the destruction such a team would cause if it were ever assembled.

Except the team wouldn't dominate from day one. They may be the world's best players, but they would still need time to gel, learn each other's movements and cover each other's gaps. Meanwhile, a team with marginally fewer talented players who had been playing together since the age of 17 at a club with a long-established philosophy, may well be able to compete with this all-star eleven.

This is the essence of succession planning; the structuring of an organisation to enable success to be sustained over time. This helps save costs, create a culture and build a legacy.

We can take some lessons from international football on this subject. Which senior European teams have had the most players come through under-17 or under-19 sides? In other words, which countries have been the best at collectively bringing talent through the system?

The first take-away from 21st Club's research is that the bigger you are, the harder it is to succession plan effectively. Picking the right 17 or 19-year-olds from a large pool is much harder than from a small pool, but it is by no means a binding factor if the right talent identification mechanisms are in place; Germany and Spain have certainly shown that.

Elsewhere, smaller nations like Wales and Switzerland, both of whom have considerably increased their FIFA ranking in recent years, have also been adept at spotting, nurturing and rewarding talent. It can be dangerous to confuse cause and effect – chopping and changing is always going to be associated with weaker talent – but with the right structures in place we can shift the odds of producing great players in our favour.

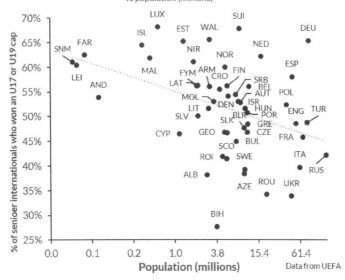

The equivalent teams at domestic level are clubs such as Schalke, Southampton, Athletic Club and Lyon, all of whom have shown how good succession planning can help you compete with those with bigger resources.

Why not take the time to look at your under-17s and ask: in 10 years' time, will succession planning mean that we are greater than the sum of our parts?

The Succession Planning Blind Spot

In 2014, Stanford University released a report detailing the attitudes of corporate executives and directors towards succession planning and talent development.

One of the more striking findings highlighted a blind spot that persists at board room level: 50% of the study's interviewees believed their board had an effective succession plan in place for senior positions, but only 25% felt that their business had an adequate pool of successors for key C-suite roles.

In the world of football, this might translate as follows:

50% of directors feel that their club is well-structured and has a succession plan in place, and would be fine in the event of key players being injured or sold, but only 25% felt that the club had an adequate pool of young players from which to draw replacements.

Clearly, it's dangerous to hold such beliefs. An effective succession plan cannot exist without a capable group of successors. Research from the corporate world suggests that it is not uncommon to hold these conflicting opinions, and perhaps this translated version rings true in football too. We often talk about long-term plans, but fail to develop the tools required to execute them. The vision is easier to formulate than the process.

Ultimately, and somewhat perversely, the corporate executives who know they have neither an effective succession plan nor an adequate pool of successors are better placed to act than those who failed to recognise that their plans were hollow. Is football any different?

The Grey Swans

Consider each of the following events:

1. The creation of a European Super League, leading to the collapse of domestic television rights.

2. A severe and sudden decline in attendances owing to demographic changes and the rise of other forms of live entertainment.

3. The removal of transfer fees through legal challenges from FIFPro.

4. The Chinese Super League attracting dozens of top division peak-age European footballers.

Each of these events might be considered a 'grey swan', an unlikely but significant event that could be anticipated but not forecast. They are the earthquakes of the football world, and in some cases the foreshocks have already taken place.

Events like the Bosman ruling, or Roman Abramovich's purchase of Chelsea, had profound effects on the world game, but not many would have predicted their occurrence or impact in the months or years before.

It might seem trivial to think about these events in the midst of a busy season, but smart clubs already have them in mind. They're wondering how, in the event of significant change, they could position themselves to take advantage of those clubs wedded to the structures of the 'old' ways.

There will be other grey swans, some specific to your own club. Quietly planning for them might be the cheapest gamble you ever make.

Even the Best Plans

In 1994, a group of psychology students nearing the end of their honours thesis were asked how long they thought their project would take to submit. Just 30% finished in their predicted time, and the average prediction was 22 days short.

In 2002, US homeowners who were remodelling their kitchens were asked how much they thought the task would cost. Their average estimate was $18,658. The actual cost averaged at $36,769.

In 2005, the budget for the 2012 London Olympics was estimated to be £2.4 billion. Just two years later, the budget was revised to £9.3 billion; a fourfold increase.

Similarly, in football, even the best plans in the world will not come to fruition exactly as you intended. Things will change, players will come-and-go, get injured, or not realise their full potential. Others may surprise you; hopefully a product of your long-term investment in youth. This is unpredictability is part of what makes football great. If everything went as forecast, then working in the game would surely be less interesting.

Despite football's mercurial nature, when planning we must always be thinking about the big picture and begin with the end in mind. Can we visualise the future? What type of club do we want to be? What does success look like for us? And how can we measure it?

By crystallising your blueprint for success, it becomes much easier to figure out contingencies when unforeseen things happen. Part of the plan is accepting that things hardly ever go to plan.

In Defence of Decisions

Decision-making in football is a thankless task. Such is the diversity of opinion that even sensible actions – selling an ageing player, for example – are likely to attract criticism. The media narrative is often deliberately contrarian and fans can be passionate beyond reason. Inaction, no matter how sensible or justified, can also cause an unwanted stir.

The effect is a lot of noise, making it hard for boardrooms to maintain a clear head and to sort the helpful, constructive criticism from the vitriol. Ultimately, this can undermine the robustness of the decision-making process, leading to mistakes born out of muddled thinking.

While it is impossible to remove the peripheral noise from the process entirely, clever use of appropriate data can at least anchor any discussion in objectivity. Like a GPS, data can tell us where we are and where we have been. This can help align stakeholders and provide an evidence-based starting point for discussions.

For example, analytics can give us an objective assessment of how efficiently our wage bill is being deployed through measuring cost against productivity. Such analysis can provide an ideal starting point in discussing which players are critical to the club's future.

This is not to say that intelligent use of data will stop all criticism; people will offer their opinions regardless, and you need to add your own context to derive maximum value. What data can do, however, is provide us with some objective evidence on which to base our judgements, thereby increasing our confidence in the decision-making process. Not only will this make our decisions easier to defend, it will make them better.

Better decisions in the boardroom will improve success on the field and, ultimately, that is the best way to bring everyone on side.

In Defence of Intuition

Intuition has historically been a decision-maker's best friend in business and sport. However, the rise of data has seen the value of intuition seemingly diminish. Data has become an objective challenger to the notion that we're capable of understanding something immediately, without the need for conscious reasoning or numbers.

The commonly held assumption that intuition is nothing more than pure guesswork perpetuates such beliefs, when in fact intuition is about feeling, sensing and pattern-matching based on past experience. The distinction is important.

It's true that snap judgments based on heuristics can represent a huge blind spot in any decision-making process, but invariably intuition leads us to ask the right questions or provide context to our data.

Intuition is good. It's even better if it's challenged by – or supplemented with – smart data.

Giving Ourselves Too Much Credit

At the end of the season, when reviewing what went right or wrong, it's often easy to pinpoint a few crucial moments. We might think that the decision to give a player a new contract provided him with added motivation for the rest of the season, or that the crisis meeting we held in December got our campaign back on track.

Invariably, these explanations will focus on our own contributions and are tinted with hindsight bias; it's simply human nature. Take a 2015 poll by YouGov which asked people in different countries who they felt contributed most to the defeat of Germany in World War Two.

Respondents in the United States overwhelmingly said that they were the biggest contributors. This was in stark contrast to British participants, who largely credited themselves with the achievement.

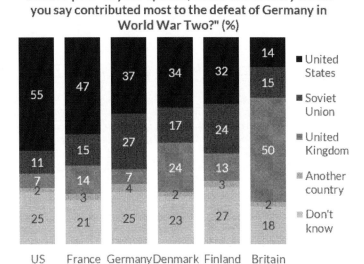

YouGov poll: "In your opinion, which one country would you say contributed most to the defeat of Germany in World War Two?" (%)

We naturally like to think about the positive impact we had on our team. However, in recognising that outcomes are often the result of processes too complex to be distilled to single decisions or moments, we can gain a better appreciation of why things happened. There is always a broader context.

The crisis meeting, for example, may have had some effect, but what about the early cup exit that refocused minds? Or the refereeing decision that went our way? How about the freak injury or suspension that gave a home-grown player a chance to prove himself? Or even the spell of great weather that helped the new player settle in?

Understanding the context behind our successes and failures is crucial to long term planning. If we give ourselves too much credit, we can create blind spots on the road ahead.

The Outside View

In his brilliant book *Thinking, Fast and Slow*, author Daniel Kahneman recalls a time when he assembled an expert team to write a textbook designed to teach judgement and decision-making in high schools.

As part of the process, Kahneman asked everyone in the team to write down an estimate of how long it would take them to submit a finished draft of the textbook to the Ministry of Education. To mitigate the perils of social proofing, Kahneman collected each prediction confidentially. The team were broadly aligned in their predictions; the low end was one and a half years, the high end two and a half years.

The discussion didn't end there. An adapted version of the conversation follows:

Kahneman: *Can you think of other teams similar to ours that had developed a curriculum from scratch?*

Seymour [the main curriculum expert on the team]: *Yes, I can think of quite a few.*

Kahneman: *From the teams who had made similar early progress as we have, how long – from that point onwards – did it take them to finish their project?*

Seymour [now blushing]: *You know, I never realised it before, but a substantial proportion – maybe 40% – of the teams failed to finish the job.*

Kahneman: *OK. Those who finished; how long did it take them?*

Seymour: *I cannot think of any group that finished in less than seven years, nor any that took more than ten.*

Kahneman: *When you compare our skills and resources to the other groups, how would you rank us?*

Seymour: *We're below average, but not by much.*

In turns out that making accurate predictions and setting realistic targets is tough. Kahneman's group had adopted what he called an 'inside view', an independent estimate based solely on our own experiences. In these situations, teams tend to optimistically or irrationally envisage best-case scenarios rather than reaching realistic evaluations.

In football it's even harder to predict the likelihood of future events, given the prevalence of known unknowns (such as player injuries) and the fact that success is often dictated by the performance of others given the interdependent nature of football leagues.

Football clubs can learn from Kahneman's experience that it is important to take an outside view when making future forecasts. Clubs should set realistic expectations for the season by establishing the prevailing circumstances and using benchmark information from similar past incidences. Historically, clubs assumed that wages determine league table position, but 21st Club have since challenged that notion by demonstrating that money doesn't always buy you success.

As we plan for the future, we can start to ask what it is we can do differently to outthink teams who are in a similar position to us.

The Red Team

Imagine having a group of people repeatedly telling you that your club is not as well-run as you think. That your player recruitment strategy is flawed. That your league status is vulnerable. That your rivals are finding new technologies and approaches to get an edge.

Now imagine that these aren't your fans; these are people that you're paying to tell you this and you welcome this attack on your business plan.

In industries outside of sport, this is known as a 'Red Team'.

Red Teams are used extensively in military and security testing, with organisations employing groups of individuals to poke holes in their systems. Importantly, they are independent of the day-to-day running of the business, often unbeknownst to most employees. They attempt to hack past defences, or act as enemies would on a battlefield, and can therefore provide insights that wouldn't necessarily be seen from the inside.

Football clubs are particularly prone to social proofing, with few people willing to challenge the preconceived ideas that have seeped into everyday processes. But what if your club recruited a Red Team? What if this team was tasked with pointing out every flaw in your strategy, and how your opponents are currently outsmarting you in various strategic areas?

Sometimes we benefit from hearing from an outside view. At critical times in the season, when decisions are often made on instinct alone, a contrarian group of opinions can help ensure that all blind spots are covered.

12 Angry Men

The classic 1957 film *12 Angry Men* tells the story of a diverse group of jurors as they deliberate over the guilt of a young defendant accused of murdering his father. The jury are all male, mostly middle-aged, white and middle-class, yet have very different personalities and character traits. Some of the men are more assertive, others more subservient; some driven by facts, others by feelings. The movie is set almost exclusively inside the jury room as the twelve men are tasked with reaching a unanimous decision.

As they enter the room, it soon becomes apparent that the jurors have already decided that the boy is guilty and wish to wrap things up quickly and return to their daily lives. All except one, that is, who is the sole "not guilty" vote in the preliminary tally. The dissenting juror goes on to explain that there is just too much at stake for him to simply go along with the verdict without at least talking about it first. The remainder of the film is then focused on the nonconformist juror challenging the personal prejudices of the others and calmly convincing them that the case is not as clear as it had initially seemed in court.

The parallels between *12 Angry Men* and any departmental meeting or boardroom decision-making process are uncanny.

The compelling, confrontational story explores the deep-rooted personal prejudices, perceptual biases, blind spots, snap judgements, cultural differences, ignorance and fears that cause the men to ignore the facts and taint their ability to make a balanced decision. It demonstrates the power of social-proofing in group dynamics and offers a brilliant lesson in consensus-building by influencing others.

Perhaps the best aspect of the movie is that there is no indication throughout as to whether the boy is actually guilty; it's irrelevant to the purpose of the film. Instead, the principal lesson is that things are usually not as obvious as they initially appear and that considering all the various information from a range of perspectives will eventually lead us to make better-informed decisions.

Tomorrow's Giants Are Today's Innovators

Football's emotive pull means that when things are going well, our club feels unstoppable. When things are going badly, we can feel hopeless. There's rarely any middle ground.

It is the same in business. Imagine working for one of the largest companies in the world just over 100 years ago. Growth and continued market dominance would have seemed inevitable. However, over half of the world's largest hundred firms in 1912 had disappeared by the end of the century, either through bankruptcy, acquisition or nationalisation. Few people working at those businesses would have predicted such a fall.

Of course, even the most dedicated strategist in football would not be planning 100 years into the future, but the unpredictability of the sport is still apparent using shorter time-frames. When comparing the league tables in England's top four divisions in 2010 to the rankings in 2015, 17 different clubs – nearly one in five – have fallen more than 20 places down the ladder. A total of eight different clubs have risen more than 20 places.

It's hard to stay at the top, and for the very best the only way is down. This should give hope to clubs who are struggling and disillusioned by the growing inequality in the game. Southampton and West Ham United finished 2014 in the top six positions of the Premier League, demonstrating that – with some innovation – it is possible to mix with the big boys. Similarly, Atlético Madrid continue to compete and succeed in La Liga despite revenues nearly five times smaller than their main domestic rivals.

It's important to acknowledge that in 12, 24 or 36 months' time at least one team at the top – of the national ladder, your division, or your 'peer group' of immediate rivals – will grow complacent and vacate its perch. The more aspirational clubs will be looking for ways to take their spot. Clubs should always be trying to innovate and challenge received wisdom, because when the time comes and the giant falls, there will always be an innovator ready to fill the gap.

Thinking About Our Assets

Take a blank piece of paper and a pen. Draw a line down the centre and intersect it horizontally to produce a matrix. Label it like so:

Next, plot your players onto the matrix, according to their cost (fixed salary plus bonuses) and productivity. Your high cost, high productivity players – what we might term established talent – should appear top right, while the low cost, high productivity players – undervalued talent – will go into the bottom right box, and so on.

It's a simple and effective exercise to help us understand how much value for money we get from our player assets. It can also be a useful starting point when reviewing the equality of the payroll and negotiating contract renewals.

Shut the Door, Take a Seat

For the majority of clubs, the end of the season triggers often uncomfortable discussions with players and their representatives as decisions are made to release players or renew their contracts. Ideally we would have made inroads into this process earlier in the campaign to avoid such a crescendo, although in reality we know it's not always possible.

There are several ways in which we can make these conversations and decisions more objective and unbiased, including:

- Processes for predicting potential

- Ways to understand the optimum age profile of the squad, and

- Methods for assessing a player's productivity against their cost

These tools support enhanced decision-making and help you to better explain the logic to players. Non-quantitative information naturally plays a major role as well, as often some of the most important contributions are the hardest to measure.

We naturally like to think about the positive impact we had on our team. However, in recognising that outcomes are often the result of processes too complex to be distilled into single decisions, we can gain a better appreciation of why things happened. There is always a broader context.

It might not make the conversation any easier, but bringing data into the heart of the discussion will make it fairer and ensure that you're making the right call.

The Flexibility-Stability Trade-Off

The difficulties in managing the contractual position of a squad are one of the main obstacles to achieving long-term success at a football club.

Buyout clauses, extension options and achievement-based pay rises are just some of the factors that must be considered within the wider context of helping the team win in the long run.

Thanks to analysis by Ben Torvaney, it has been shown that the twenty-four clubs in the English Championship in 2014/15 took varied approaches to managing their contracts, illustrating the trade-off that exists between flexibility and stability.

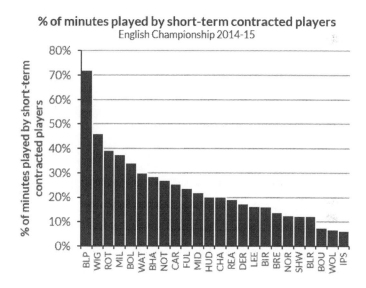

% of minutes played by short-term contracted players
English Championship 2014-15

Many clubs nearer the bottom of the league, unsure of their ultimate fate, opted to sign and field players on short-term deals. Other clubs nearer the top of the division persisted with the players who, in many cases, brought at least satisfactory results last season.

Clearly, it would be dangerous to assume any causal link between stability and success. It seems unlikely that teams are near the bottom of the league because of their contractual flexibility. Instead, it's more likely a conscious choice given their circumstances, those teams hoping to remain mobile should the worst-case scenario arise. However, the data helps us ask whether having more options during the season – and accepting that it will give us more headaches afterwards – is a trade-off worth entertaining.

Regardless of the contractual position that a club takes, strategic long-term planning – with a full understanding of the possible unknowns on the horizon – is essential to ensuring that flexibility does not equal chaos, nor stability stagnation.

A Framework for Squad Evolution

The January transfer window is very much 'Level 2' in the game that is transfer business. Gone are the summer comforts of infrequent matches and ample negotiating time, replaced instead by injuries, premium prices and an all-or-nothing approach.

As such, the January transfer window arguably requires much more planning than its off-season sibling. Whilst clubs are often quick to identify the players they want, most need to make tough decisions on who to sell in order to accommodate this activity.

There are a few top-level factors to consider when making these decisions, including age, productivity and value. These can be distilled and measured against each other to provide a decision-making framework for squad evolution.

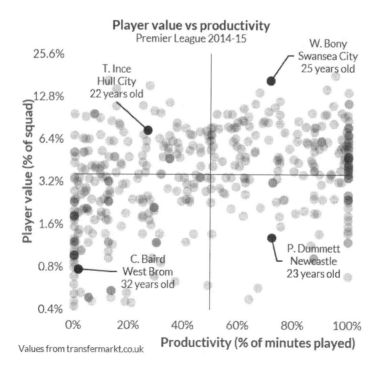

Player value vs productivity
Premier League 2014-15

Values from transfermarkt.co.uk

Most clubs would ideally see a positive correlation between their high-value (typically high-cost) players and their playing time. However, for various reasons – manager preferences, injuries, or rotation, for example – we are left with a number of high value, low productivity and low value, high productivity players.

Take high value, low productivity players. For players over the age of 23, remaining in this category for another six months may cause their value to depreciate, and thus January might be the time to cash in. What's more, these players are likely to be a bigger burden on the wage bill. Meanwhile, players aged 23 or younger in this category might be worth loaning out, for many are potential stars who perhaps need playing time to develop.

Low value, high productivity players are a mix of old pros who are probably worth retaining (if the wage bill allows) and younger players who will potentially see their own value rise through increased exposure. Perhaps these pre-peak players are the ones to lock into long-term deals.

Countless other factors such as dressing room influence, injury record and squad depth, means that there are few straightforward and all-encompassing answers. However, in the time between the start of the season and the winter window, it's essential to have a clear vision of where the value lies within your own squad and a framework for making decisions in January. Your best negotiating position is to have your own strategy in place.

The Evolution of Barcelona

In May 2008, the forecast looked bleak for FC Barcelona. The Catalan giants had finished the season 18 points behind champions Real Madrid, who had sealed back-to-back titles for the first time in nearly two decades.

We all know what happened next. Pep Guardiola was promoted from B team duties and led Barcelona to two Champions Leagues and three La Liga titles in four years, revolutionising the way we think about football in the process.

While much attention has been paid to the club's change in playing style, the squad itself underwent significant alterations during the first few seasons of Guardiola's reign. By 2010/11, just 45% of outfield minutes were played by those remaining from the 2007/08 squad, with players like Ronaldinho, Deco and Oleguer quickly dismissed.

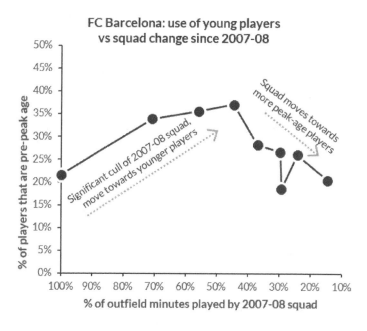

As part of this process, the first team became younger and more dynamic. The remnants of the 2007/08 team slowly eroded, save for those players developed at La Masia, Barcelona's world-renowned academy. In the last five years, much of the squad has moved into peak-age territory, with no end to the succession of titles.

It's always useful to think about your own squad evolution and where it is taking your team. Of the 20-25 first team players on your books, how many will be around in two years' time? How about in five years' time? How will the age profile of the team need to be altered in order to remain competitive?

Long-term planning needn't be prescriptive, but knowing the direction of travel is essential.

Managing Expectations: The New Season

Expectations are always high ahead of the new season as clubs look forward to a fresh start with high hopes.

The question is: how to manage them?

Setting expectations is about finding the sweet spot between optimism and realism. Set the bar too low and fans will question your ambition as a club; too high, and you risk having to explain the consequences of perceived under-achievement. This is the dilemma that football's leaders face ahead of any new season.

Come what May, success will be defined by results and league table position. Before the season, however, clubs have the opportunity to set expectations around realistic targets. Essentially, this comes down to managing preconceptions (what people think will happen) and communication (how well you describe what is likely to happen).

Preconceptions are typically formed on the basis of past results, so understanding previous benchmarks is a great starting point. By analysing the points required for success (whatever that means to your club) in your division over the past ten seasons, it is possible to set realistic and tangible points targets for your club.

Average points by league position, 2004 - 2014				
Position	Premier League	C'ship	League One	League Two
Champions	88	93	94	88
2nd	83	86	87	83
3rd	77	81	83	82
4th	70	77	80	79
6th	62	73	74	73
7th	58	71	71	71
Last survival position	37	50	50	48

Communication plays a vital role in this process. It should not be assumed that everyone is clear on the plan or what is likely to happen over the course of the season. It is important to explain to all key stakeholders – owners, players, staff and fans – what should be expected.

Managing expectations isn't necessarily about being conservative, it should be seen as a great opportunity. The most successful sports teams, products and businesses succeed because they exceed expectations in innovative ways.

The question for clubs then becomes: what are others doing to reach their expectations, and what can we do to exceed them?

Did You Exceed Expectations?

When setting expectations for the season, instead of aiming for a certain league position it is better to identify a points total as a performance benchmark. The reason for this is that while league position can be at the mercy of rivals' form, points are something within a club's control.

Take Sevilla, a club perennially on the fringes of Spain's top four, as an example. Before the 2014/15 season, the club might have looked at what it has historically taken to finish in the Champions League places. In the previous ten years, fourth place averaged 65 points, with a maximum of 70.

However, Sevilla hadn't reckoned with a resurgent Valencia who, like themselves, consistently swept aside bottom-half teams en route to their second-highest ever points total. Sevilla finished fifth with 76 points, better than most third placed teams over the last decade. Of course, Sevilla secured their Champions League place via the Europa League, but were really worth their position on league points alone.

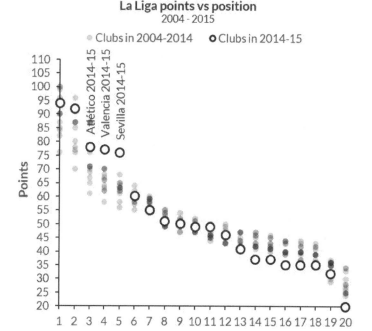

La Liga points vs position
2004 - 2015

It is important to consider changing league and opponent dynamics, but reassessing expectations relative to points is critical for effective long-term planning. A club that has fallen short on position but exceeded expectations on points may make unnecessary changes simply because the league table was an unfair reflection of their output. Similarly, a club in the opposite situation may have found themselves the beneficiaries of underachieving rivals.

Before shaping expectations for the new season, it is perhaps best to reflect on how well targets were set in the previous campaign. Were they the right expectations, and what can we do to exceed the new benchmark next season?

Bibliography

Books

Ankersen, Rasmus, *Hunger in Paradise: How to Save Success from Failure* (Turbulenz, 2013)

Kahneman, Daniel, *Thinking, Fast and Slow* (Penguin, 2012)

McKeown, Greg, *Essentialism: The Disciplined Pursuit of Less* (Crown Business, 2014)

Academic Papers

Larcker, David. F and Saslow, Scott, *2014 Report On Senior Executive Succession Planning and Talent Development* (Stanford Graduate School of Business, 2014)

Levitt, Steven. D, List, John. A, Neckermann, Susanne and Sadoff, Sally, *The Behaviouralist Goes to School: Leveraging Behavioural Economics to Improve Educational Performance* (National Bureau of Economic Research, 2012)

Newspapers

The Guardian

The Independent

The Times

Websites

www.bbc.co.uk/radio4

www.bbc.co.uk/sport

www.eloratings.net

www.espn.co.uk

www.fifa.com

www.grantland.com

www.thepowerofgoals.blogspot.co.uk

www.transfermarkt.co.uk

https://twitter.com/Torvaney (Ben Torvaney)

Films

12 Angry Men (United Artists, 1957)

Moneyball (Columbia Pictures, 2011)

EVOLUTION

The smart way to plan for the future

Software for football club boardrooms

COMING SOON

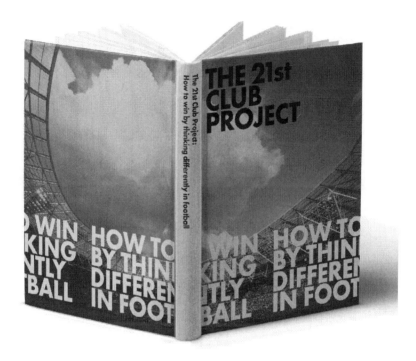

Released in 2017

17351987R00081

Printed in Great Britain
by Amazon